Praise for *Caves of Power*

'I am fascinated by the work of Sergio Magaña and have had the pleasure of working with him and learning the obsidian mirror process, which was life-changing. Sergio is a true healer and medicine man, plus he's a lot of fun. Now, in his latest book, Sergio has provided us with more keys to access our inner power to transform and heal our lives, and those of others. The instructions are simply and clearly written, so you'll be able to get started right away.'

Dr Christiane Northrup, *New York Times* bestselling author of *Goddesses Never Age*

'*Caves of Power* is Sergio Magaña's third book and undoubtedly his best! Already an eminent healer in Mexico, a reputable international teacher and acclaimed author, Sergio offers us deep layers of the unique and precious ancient knowledge of a rich Mexicayotl wisdom path that has, until now, only been passed on orally from master to student. The profound teachings in this book, which include astonishing and precise maps of the underworlds and "caves of power", the places where we can access and transform our shadows and fears, and activate our dreams and true powers, are indeed priceless during this period of transition, where we are asked to awaken, confront our shadows, heal ourselves, take our powers and evolve.'

Christa Mackinnon, author of *Shamanism and Spirituality in Therapeutic Practice*

'Once again Sergio has found a way to accessibly translate ancient Mexican wisdom for a modern audience and thus make true the prophecy of 2012. Perhaps more importantly, though, the practices he teaches actually work, so don't just read this book – practise what it teaches and manifest your innate capacity for healing.'

Charlie Morley, author of *Dreams of Awakening*

'Back in the early 70s a friend persuaded me to read Carlos Casteneda's *The Teachings of Don Juan*. I enjoyed an intriguingly good read, but it felt so far from my experience at that time that I could not integrate and use the teachings. Last year I came across *The Toltec Secret* by Sergio Magaña and found it to be an extraordinarily clear expression of what Casteneda had written about. Now here is *Caves of Power*, his third book – a clear, concise manual of how our being and the reality we live in really work, how the world we experience is constructed, and how to access deep altered states that can enable us to live in both worlds simultaneously. This work can creatively and consistently transform one's life and enable one to assist the lives of others. It has given me a series of maps to work from to develop my Self and my abilities – caves of power that I can access within myself.'

Leo Rutherford, founder of the Eagle's Wing College of Contemporary Shamanism

Praise for *The Dawn of the Sixth Sun,* also by Sergio Magaña Ocelocoyotl

'Speaking from the Náhuatl tradition, Sergio Magaña has been entrusted with the sacred task of revealing once-secret knowledge on the transformation of the Earth and humanity. The book is an instruction manual for anyone who wants to awaken from the dreamlike trance of ordinary reality and attain a truly lucid state.'
DANIEL PINCHBECK, AUTHOR OF *2012: THE RETURN OF QUETZALCÓATL*

'We have entered a period of rapid and deep-seated worldwide transformation in which each one of us needs to master the inner world of his or her own consciousness. In this book, Sergio Magaña, inheritor of this wisdom and now its spokesman, shares his uniquely precious knowledge with us. His writing deserves to become a pillar of the new-paradigm wisdom we need during the critical years that mark the Dawn of the Sixth Sun.'
ERVIN LASZLO, NOBEL PRIZE NOMINEE

'Sergio Magaña Ocelocoyotl gives us a vision of hope and inspires us to do the inner spiritual work needed for a beautiful transformation. *The Dawn of the Sixth Sun* is filled with practices that help us align with our higher selves so we can blossom into our fullness as human beings.'
SANDRA INGERMAN, AUTHOR OF *SHAMANIC JOURNEYING* AND *HOW TO THRIVE IN CHANGING TIMES*

'The ancient knowledge that Sergio Magaña shares in this book teaches us how to realign ourselves with the universe so that we can play our true role as conduits for the transition from one era of human consciousness to the next.'
DR MARILYN SCHLITZ, GLOBAL AMBASSADOR AND SENIOR SCIENTIST, INSTITUTE OF NOETIC SCIENCES

'This is a book to study. Take it seriously! In essence, Sergio says, "Clean up your act now." Other traditions have been saying this in a much more transmuted way. I am looking forward to trying the exercises.'
GAY LUCE, FOUNDER OF NINE GATES MYSTERY SCHOOL

CAVES *of* POWER

CAVES *of* POWER

Ancient Energy Techniques for Healing,
Rejuvenation and Manifestation

Sergio Magaña Ocelocoyotl

HAY HOUSE

Carlsbad, California • New York City
London • Sydney • New Delhi

The cave you fear to enter holds the treasure that you seek.

JOSEPH CAMPBELL

Contents

CONTENTS

List of Exercises

Introduction

I started to write this book today not on a computer, or even on paper, but in front of a mirror. I was looking at the lines on my face. According to the Toltec and Mexihca oral tradition, which dates back to the earlier Central American civilizations of the Chichimecas, Olmecs, Teotihuacáns and Xochicalcas, the lines on your face show everything you've ever experienced, but above all the way you've lived your life on Mother Earth.

So today I looked at the lines on my face, examining all the furrows and wrinkles from top to bottom. And I honoured them, for they represent all my experiences and all the knowledge I've acquired along the way. It is thanks to them that it is possible for me to write this book, *Caves of Power*.

So, with a smile on my face, I would like to present some of my experiences in the Toltec and Mexihca tradition and as an energy healer. And I would like to share some techniques that I hope will benefit you and help you to heal your life.

My name is Sergio Magaña Gil. I was born in the bosom of a very traditional Catholic family in Mexico City. Approximately nine years ago, when one of my teachers in the Mexihca tradition, Hugo Nahui, was calculating my mother's moon cycle, the first thing he said was: 'So Sergio is the other son.'

Part of the Mexihca tradition is based on a very accurate lunar calendar that is unknown to most people. However, Hugo is an expert on it. According to the tradition, we are ruled by different phases of the moon and this changes every three years. It is important to know which phase was ruling your parents during your gestation as well as which was ruling on the day you were born. Most people are gestated when their mother is ruled by the full moon. As a result, they have a strong attachment to the material world, to their family, religion, etc., which our society accepts as normal. But, unlike the rest of my siblings, I was gestated on the waning moon of both my parents and born on the waxing moon.

The waxing moon gives you good health and the talent and drive to succeed. It is also very good for taking knowledge from the past and presenting it in a modern way.

Children gestated under the influence of a waning moon have artistic and spiritual inclinations, but also addictive tendencies and a liking for dangerous, bizarre or even illegal situations.

My life is testament to this ancient Mexican knowledge. I have exhibited the characteristics of a child gestated under a waning moon my whole life, in many different ways, and I was doing so before I was even aware of Mexican lunar astrology.

One of the main traits of waning-moon children is an interest in the spiritual quest. My own spiritual journey started because of a coincidence. However, those of us who are on such journeys will know that there are no coincidences. On the contrary, events are perfectly synchronized to allow us to meet the people who will help us fulfil our destiny. Ultimately, we all have the same destiny, which is 'blooming' or 'blossoming', a term used by the ancient Toltecs and Mexihcas for what is known nowadays as enlightenment.

The first encounter I had with my lunar legacy was when my mother decided to study and work. Because of this, my siblings and I were mostly brought up by people who worked for my parents. I was raised by my nanny, Rosa Hernandez Monroy, known to me as Rosita. My siblings were brought up by a different nanny, also, funnily enough, named Rosa.

Rosita came from an Otomi community in San Pablo Autopan, which is very close to the city of Toluca in Mexico state, and her father was its healer. She was destined to become his successor, but she fled her home town after being brutally beaten by her husband and escaped to Mexico City barefoot and without a word of Spanish. She ended up working for my parents, and when I was born, I became the son she could never have.

So my childhood was unique, since I was effectively brought up by two mothers who loved me a lot but expressed it in very different ways: one very strictly and according to religious and scientific laws, and the other very tenderly and according to the medicine and magic of the ancient Mexican people, combined with the Catholic religion.

When I was in pain, for example, instead of giving me traditional medicine, Rosita would simply take a pack of *Delicados*, a Mexican brand of cigarettes made of pure tobacco (which of course she kept hidden, since it was strictly forbidden to smoke at home, especially in front of the children), light a cigarette and make circles with the smoke around the painful area. Then she would draw in the smoke and exhale it, and as it disappeared, the pain would disappear too. Of course she asked me to keep this a secret, as she would probably have been fired if my parents had found out.

Rosita was also the first person to talk to me about the importance of dreams. When I had what most people call nightmares, she would say, 'I am going to clean you with an egg.' When I asked why, she told me something I've never forgotten: 'An egg symbolizes a dream that will never come true. The dream of this egg is to become a chicken, and that will never happen. So I'm going to use it to prevent your bad dreams from coming true.'

She would pass the egg over parts of my body, making counterclockwise circles with it. Then she would break it, pour it into a glass of water and read the patterns formed by the white and yolk.

So I learned the art of healing with tobacco and an egg, and although I don't use those methods anymore, they contributed to the development of my healing skills and my interactions with the world of energy. I was also initiated into the art of dreaming without knowing it.

I believe that these lessons from Rosita laid the basis for my future career as an energy healer. They showed me two things: i) conventional medicine wasn't the only way to heal physical and emotional problems; and ii) dreams were important because they would manifest in waking reality, but if you didn't like a dream, you could change it.

Another important technique I learned from Rosita was how to change my perception of the world around me. As a child I was very shy and insecure, and people, starting with my brother, would often take advantage of me. So Rosita gave me a piece of advice: 'When you feel helpless in the face of external attacks, move your eyes sideways.' Now I understand she was referring to peripheral vision. When you move your eyes sideways at a very pronounced angle, you can make what we know as reality disappear from view.

I did this a lot of times when I was a child – when my parents told me off, when my classmates bothered me, and so on – and I entered a world in which it was impossible for me to react or feel hurt. Literally, I escaped reality.

Unfortunately, when I became a teenager, I stopped practising this technique. When people bothered me, I reacted negatively instead. Full of fear and anger, I created an insecure and addictive personality that I struggled with for a long time.

I would like to point out something very important here: I learned to heal others amazingly effectively before I learned to heal myself. For this reason, I firmly believe that if you apply the correct techniques, you can become a great healer even when your own life is a mess. I am emphasizing this point since I have heard a lot of people say, 'First I need to heal myself, then I can heal others.' In the end, this is simply an excuse not to heal others and not to heal yourself either – in other words, self-sabotage. In my case, I consider that healing so many people before healing myself generated favourable winds, as they say in the energetic tradition. That is, it generated good energy that subsequently not only allowed me to heal myself but also thousands of other people. Had I waited to heal myself first, nothing would have happened.

Another great advantage of growing up in Rosita's care was that as I was using my peripheral vision to make reality disappear, I was looking at the world from a lower angle, which allowed me to see people's energy fields. So my brain got used to it. Nevertheless, I also stopped doing this for many years and only took it up again when life presented me with a series of events that forced me to do so.

The second distinctive feature of children gestated under the waning moon is a love of the arts, something which became clearly evident in my life. From childhood, I loved movies and the theatre and dreamed of becoming an actor. When I left school, that was all I wanted to do. But at that time, 20 years ago, allowing a son to become an actor was inconceivable for a traditional Mexican family. There were a lot of irrational prejudices against the artistic environment. It was considered degenerate, even dangerous, and unlikely to provide enough money to live on. As a result, my parents thwarted my dramatic aspirations by every means available and forced me to study a more practical subject instead.

At the time, I was totally frustrated by this. For years, I felt my family had wrecked my life. Now I see it as the turning point that led me to what I believe is my destiny, since it triggered the third characteristic of children gestated under a waning moon: a taste for bizarre and dangerous things.

I began rebelling against the rules – any rules. Although this made my life very complicated, today I am very grateful for it. It was the only way for me to learn never to accept any impositions on my personal life, or any medical diagnosis, or have any preconceptions about my patients. Eventually it allowed me to perform many healings that modern science would consider impossible. And later I was very successful at developing methods of rejuvenation.

In the meantime, the way I escaped reality changed from moving my eyes to drinking, taking drugs and partying. Of course this lifestyle didn't go down well with a strict Catholic family and a mother obsessed with discipline, and it resulted in my father punishing me and even throwing me out of the house. Luckily, I always had good friends who helped me out in hard times and put me up when necessary. Fortunately I never had to experience anything that could really have damaged my life or my moral integrity. And in spite of my mother's verbal aggressiveness towards me, she did have a key point when she said, 'Like St Augustine, your spirituality will save you.'

I also have to recognize that in her own way she really made a great effort to help me. She made me go to many different therapists, including a psychologist. Of course there are no coincidences in life, and the psychologist she sent me to, Laura Muñoz, became my first official energy teacher. I'm infinitely grateful to her. When I first went to her, she diagnosed me according to what she saw in my aura, and so I realized she used peripheral vision too. At the time I still wanted to be an actor, but she said, 'You're going to be a healer like me – a very good one.'

Besides offering individual healing sessions, Laura also gave courses on many subjects, including healing with energy, fire and candles, and using a pendulum. With her, my interest in spiritual things revived and I started to gain confidence when I saw that I could relieve people of physical pain, manifest things and perform distance healing.

However, as I mentioned before, I was able to heal others long before I was able to heal myself, and I continued my reckless party lifestyle until my parents threw me out for the last time. Then I was forced to support myself.

I started working in a bar and lived quite a simple life so that I could indulge my passion for partying. Looking back, those were hard times really – full of fun, but at the same time very destructive.

One day a friend of mine invited me to a talk on nutritional products. There were four people there apart from my friend and me. The talk started out being about nutrients, but all of a sudden it changed into a discussion of alternative medicine, and at one point I asked one of the other people, 'Do you happen to have had surgery around the navel?'

She answered, 'Yes, a Caesarean, but how do you know?'

As I have already told you, changing my perception allowed me to see other people's energy fields. And when you undergo surgery, the energy channels, the meridians, of your body are also cut. Not many people know this, but those who are able to see the energetic field closest to the body can identify where surgery has been performed because they can see an abnormal yellowish accumulation of energy around that area. As time goes by, this produces problems.

So I said, 'I can see the energy accumulating in that spot.'

Wide-eyed, her friend stood in front of me and asked, 'What about me?'

I looked at her energy and said, 'You've had surgery on your legs.'

She couldn't believe her ears. She explained she'd had multiple operations because she had a lot of circulatory problems in her legs.

Another of her friends, who was wearing a turtle-necked sweater, asked in a sceptical tone, 'And me?'

I said simply, 'On the neck.'

This was also true, since she had had a biopsy and an operation on her thyroid gland.

When I explained about the accumulation of energy, they all asked, 'Can you heal it?'

I replied, 'Yes, I can fix it,' and I wasn't lying, as I'd learned from Laura how to repair meridians. The next thing was they were making appointments for healing sessions with me. So that was the beginning of my career as a healer.

What I didn't know at the time was that one of them was the subdirector of a centre for behavioural problems in Mexico City and very soon she started sending all her patients to me for meridian reconstruction. Within a month, my appointments diary was full every day of the week.

It was then that my mother's words came to mind: 'Like St Augustine, your spirituality will save you.' So I quit my job at the bar, though not the partying – that was something I was only able to do a long time later.

In the healing sessions, people felt an incredible flow of energy. Soon I was in demand. I quickly became aware that my knowledge was really quite limited. However, Rosita's teachings had always been very useful, so I used those, and I was really good at lucid dreaming, so in my lucid dreams I asked for information, techniques and symbols to solve health, abundance and relationship problems. I also started taking advantage of the moment immediately after I woke up to ask what I called my higher consciousness for new therapies. At the time I thought this was channelling; now I know I was contacting the unconscious – in the ancient Mexican tradition, the caves of power.

Afterwards, I tried out the results of my research on my patients. I must confess that I was sceptical. I wasn't self-confident at all.

But the healing was very effective. I ought to have been happy, but I somehow felt guilty because of the way I was living my life and because I was different from what I imagined a healer to be. It was hard to believe I was actually healing people so easily and so effectively, and yet it was happening. With all the recommendations, each month my diary was full.

Here another noteworthy lesson came to me: if you are given information in a lucid dream that goes beyond what you know, have confidence in it, whatever is happening in the waking world. It will deliver concrete results. I was experiencing that with my patients every day.

Then I took the next step. The woman who had sent me all her patients asked me if I could teach them my healing techniques, and I agreed. Soon afterwards, I found myself teaching my first course at the centre for behavioural problems.

I had eight attendees and it turned out that one of them had a radio show on mystical and astrological topics. She offered to interview me. Afterwards, the audience went so crazy that the radio station offered me my own show. Believe it or not, three months later I had my own show on the radio.

Looking back, I understand now that what happened then was part of my destiny. It propelled me into my life plan, which was necessary, because personally I was making no effort to get started with it.

Radio shows are very good ways to advertise in Mexico; soon after mine started, I had courses packed with 80 to

100 attendees and multiple assistants. Obviously, I was also making a lot of money. My courses grew even larger thanks to the astonishing testimonials of my students on the radio programme *2010: Ahead of Time*. They talked about recovering from 'incurable' diseases, making radical changes in their lives and, most striking of all, rejuvenating. Two years later, I had approximately 2,000 to 3,000 students on my courses each solstice and equinox, as well as hundreds of students on my weekly courses, and was touring different cities in Mexico, such as Monterrey, Guadalajara and Veracruz.

The life I was living was awesome. People were kissing my hand as if I were a saint, waiting for me outside hotels, following me and sending me e-mails about how they had been healed.

The situation got out of control when an important politician called me. He was very sick and wanted me to go to his place to heal him, but I asked him to make an appointment like anyone else. Next thing I knew, he'd sent a party of bodyguards who forced me to go and heal him.

I started to be scared by all the attention, and I was worn out as well. So I tried to get away from it all by throwing myself into my social life. Here and now I would like to apologize for all the times I was late for my courses and didn't fulfil my commitments. I was living a life that was beyond my control and my mind couldn't process it.

On the one hand, I was healing people and was receiving thousands of letters and expressions of gratitude. On the other, I hadn't been able to change my personal life at all. I was still hanging out with friends, going to nightclubs and letting people down as a result. It wasn't all negative, though, because it made me feel normal, worldly. I guess that was actually why I remained grounded. Unlike so many people on the spiritual path, I never felt superior to others, I simply recognized that I had a special talent to work with. Actually, I felt pretty uncomfortable with all the flattery, gifts and mail. I longed to escape from the spiritual world and fulfil my dream of becoming an actor.

I strongly believe that the events of our lives have already been planned in the collective dream by the Great Grandmother Spider, who has woven all our destinies in her invisible web. And it was at this point that the teacher I mentioned to you before, Hugo García or Hugo Nahui (his name in the ancient language of Mexico), an expert on dreams and lunar astrology, came into my life.

Hugo had spent years studying self-development and many forms of spirituality, including the Bible, the Kabbalah, astrology and the Mexihca tradition. I see him as a modern Renaissance man. At the time, he was driving a bus for a living and was determined to teach only those who got on the bus. One day I got on. How? He heard my radio programme and, after listening to me for a while, realized that I was the person who would spread his message. He started attending my courses as a student and then one day he confessed, 'I'm not here to learn, but to teach you.'

He started giving me private lessons every week. He taught me about lucid dreaming, the Mexihca culture and the Toltec tradition without charging me a cent, so I realized his intention was genuine. It was thanks to him that I developed an absolute passion for all the ancient traditions of Mexico. My real transformation was about to start.

One day he made a prophecy: 'After the eclipse of 11 July 2010, the Mexihca knowledge will spread worldwide and you will be one of the spokespeople for it.'

When he said this, all I knew were the teachings of my Otomi nanny, my lucid dreaming practices and the basics of the Mexihca and Toltec tradition, so I didn't pay too much attention to it. He also said, 'You will start in Italy and then move to England,' which seemed unlikely at the time. But I didn't question him, I just forgot about it. Now, many years later, I can see he was right, as everything has unfolded exactly as he said.

Shortly after Hugo came into my life, the radio station suddenly decided to cancel my contract. I felt relieved and, since I didn't need to work, I decided to take some time off and disappear from public view for a while. No more courses, no more healing. My healing school kept running, though, thanks to the people I had trained earlier.

At the time, I was having the same lucid dream over and over: Popocatépetl, the most sacred mountain in Mexico, kept telling me, 'You have to go to the Andes mountains to learn how to work with the Mexican mountains.'

So I started to go to Cusco and Huasao, in Peru, to learn the tradition of the Andean shamans, the *paqos*. I met a woman called Vilma Pinedo, who became a great friend of mine, and it turned out that she and her family were heirs to one of the most outstanding lineages of Andean knowledge. I will always be grateful to Vilma and her family for teaching me their sacred knowledge.

Later on, Hugo said to me, 'I would like to introduce you to my friend Xolotl, so that he can continue teaching you.'

And so it was that I met one of the most important people of my life. Xolotl is one of most exceptional teachers I've ever known, and one whom I honour, as I do the rest of my teachers. He gave me private lessons every Tuesday for years, instructing me in Aztec and Toltec cosmology and dance, Náhuatl, the pre-Hispanic language of Mexico, and nahualism, the ancient Mexican dreaming tradition. Both his lessons and the ones I'd already learned gave meaning to my life. For the first time I felt I was doing the right thing. This was where I belonged – it was my real role in life, not the ones I'd been playing through chance, necessity or ambition.

Finally, after thousands of testimonials about transforming the lives of others, I realized I had to transform my own. I started lucid dreaming and working with the obsidian mirror, an ancient Mexican technique, to heal my own 'cave', my inner self or unconscious, and eventually my life changed dramatically. I went back to live with my parents for a year and was able to heal the wounds of childhood and adolescence. I was determined not to let the past ruin my future and I was able to heal a large part of myself during this time. It's a never-ending process of course, and I'm still working on it.

I hadn't been able to leave my old lifestyle behind until I'd found something much better to do, but now I had: dreaming. Dreaming within a tradition, rather than experimentally, as I had before. I began exploring the heavens and the underworlds of the Toltec tradition, meeting ancestors and discovering what actually takes place during the hours when most people are totally unconscious. Believe me when I tell you that what happens when you're dreaming is much more interesting than what happens when you're awake.

I took the decision not to lose my mind while I was asleep *or* awake. And since then, although I still hang out with friends and sometimes I drink, I've never lost consciousness or control. As I wrote in my previous book, *The Toltec Secret*, 'The ancient Mexican tradition … saved my life and now I have devoted my life to rescuing it.'

Full of determination, I went back to work, to the radio and to public life. But I had changed deep inside. I had decided never to do healing again and to stop teaching simple healing techniques. Instead I would simply teach the Mexihca and Andean traditions. So I revolutionized the format of the radio show. The Toltec and Mexihca traditions in particular, are complex and demand discipline. You have to face your demons and to cultivate lucid dreams, and the results are rewarding only after years of practice, not after two days.

As might be expected, the people who had been waiting for me to return were startled; it was a different person's programme and I lost most of my followers. But it was simple: I had changed and my students had to do so too.

Everybody advised me to go back to the old formula, but I couldn't help thinking that if I went back, I would die. I didn't care that I was using up all my savings financing my new radio programme – I was determined to take the risk. In the past, I'd done the programme to raise money; now I was making an offering of all my money and my confidence to succeed in my new programme.

I felt I was doing the right thing, in contrast to the past, when I'd been conspicuously successful but hadn't felt that I was acting correctly and had experienced a huge emptiness as a result. But my family and friends kept telling me that my new project wouldn't work because Mexicans weren't interested in anything related to their country: they were Malinchistas, a term related to Malinalli, Hernán Cortés' interpreter, who was blamed for a large part of the fall of the Aztec Empire, and they only ever liked what came from overseas.

These claims made me angry because they were partly true. I thought, *It's so illogical to have this beautiful and rich tradition in our country and keep looking overseas for knowledge when it's hidden right here!*

I was determined to make our own traditions known. I started lucid dreaming in order to become successful with what I was doing, and though I didn't reach the same heights as in the past, I managed to make my programme a hit again. People came on my courses too, but obviously they were different from before. People who were looking for a guru who would save them were replaced by people who were determined to take their destiny into their own hands.

Once again, testimonials of miraculous healings and extraordinarily deep transformations flooded in. However, this time I wasn't responsible for them. I was only the means. Those concerned had done it all on their own. Often I was amazed by what had happened. It was my students who taught me what could be achieved with the techniques I taught.

I was no longer facing the hassle of unwanted attention and demands. I simply felt like a member of the tribe, of the *calpulli*, as important as anyone else, and as unimportant as well.

It was then that Hugo's prophecy came true. And everything happened so easily, just as with my first radio programme. An Italian editor offered to publish my first book, *The Dawn of the Sixth Sun*, then later Hay House in the UK published the second one, *The Toltec Secret*, and I started sharing the ancient Mexican traditions with the rest of the world through my courses. As Hugo had said, I started in Italy and then moved to England.

I must confess that this was actually pretty tough, because it was just when I had finally achieved stability in all aspects in my life in Mexico that I started travelling all over the world. I suffered a lot of depression during the first two years and felt tempted to go back home. People told me I was making much more money in Mexico and was better off there. But that would have been a step backwards and, as before, something inside me said, 'You are doing the right thing.' So once again I was loyal to myself and went on.

Today I'm writing the end of this introduction in Istanbul, after a wonderful course of obsidian mirror work and some beautiful days here. I know now that although I suffered a lot in the beginning, everything has been worthwhile. Amazing places, extraordinary people. I look again at the lines on my face and smile. Everything has been so rewarding.

Hugo taught me that 'Mexico' meant 'the place of the moon's navel' and that being a Mexihca didn't refer to being Mexican, but being a person who paid attention to their dreams and endeavoured to change them. These Mexihca teachings are not just for Mexicans, but for all those seekers around the world who believe that a miracle can happen if they dream a new dream.

That's why I'm writing this new book. It's a compilation of the lessons I've learned throughout my life: from Rosita, Laura, Hugo, Xolotl, the *paqos* in the Andes and my own dreams. Much of what is written here is Mexico's real treasure: its wisdom.

In ancient Mexico, *nahual* was the name given to the wise man or woman who was able to merge the dream state and the waking state either awake or asleep. In my last book, I outlined some methods of doing this while asleep. In this new book, I will describe some methods of doing it in a conscious state. I will also reveal some very practical techniques to help you become responsible for your own destiny and heal the collective unconscious.

In line with the cosmic mathematics of the ancient Mexicans, I will present this information in four sections: healing, rejuvenation, manifestation and blooming or enlightenment.

These are some of the things you may achieve if you succeed in knowing your inner self, your 'caves of power'.

Join me on this journey and discover the power within, and believe me, if you apply what you learn to yourself and others, you will completely transform your life.

I wish you well on your journey to self-knowledge.

Sergio Magaña Ocelocoyotl

Chicome Ocelotl, Atemoztli, Xihuitl Yei Acatl
Day Seven, Jaguar score, the subsiding waters, Year Three Reed
19 January 2016
London, United Kingdom

PART I

Healing

Chapter i

The Human Energy System

If we wish to follow the ancient Mexican way of healing, first we have to become familiar with our energy system. This is generally known as the aura, the energy surrounding us, and the chakras (Sanskrit *cakra*, 'wheel'), our energy centres. These concepts have parallels in the ancient Mexican tradition, which has five bodies and seven energy centres.

Five Bodies

Just as we need five fingers on each of our hands for them to work as a whole, so we need five bodies to express our full physical, mental and spiritual capacities. These are:

- *tonacayo*, the physical body

    This is the body that allows us to experience material reality.

- *ihiyotl*, 'encouragement' or 'life force', the subtle energy that comes from the etheric worlds and helps keep matter in motion

This energy is connected to us through our liver and our legs. The ancient Mexicans explained the death process as follows: 'Death happens when the *ihiyotl* leaves the body and then the physical body is motionless.' (This process does not include the energy bodies, which go their own way.)

~ *teyolia*, the energy that surrounds the heart

This is the energy in which our whole life experience resides throughout our life, or lives, and even in our dreams. It holds and therefore keeps creating our most deeply rooted emotional and behavioural patterns.

In ancient Egypt, the equivalent of the *teyolia* was the *ba*.

~ *tonal*, the energy that surrounds the head while we are awake

The term *tonal* is related to heat, daylight and the sun. Today it is known as our mind and personality.

Those who have developed extrasensory perception can see the *tonal* as an amber halo around the head. When it is around the head, we feel more aware of material reality, with its laws of time and space. When we sleep, it moves from the head to the abdominal area, swapping locations with the next body, the *nahual*.

~ *nahual*, the energy body that we use while asleep and also one of the vehicles that we will use after death

This term comes from the Náhuatl *nehua*, meaning 'I', and *nahualli*, 'what extends'. So together they mean 'who I am beyond the *tonal* and material reality'. The *nahual* is governed by the moon.

As I mentioned earlier, the *nahual* and *tonal* change places when we sleep. When the *nahual* reaches our head, we are able to use another means of perception: dreaming. In the world of dreams, there is no time and there are no physical constraints. For the ancient Mexicans, this was where everything in the waking world was created.

In ancient Egypt, the equivalent of the *nahual* was the *ka*.

The movement of all of these bodies forms the aura, or energy sphere, also known as *teotolontli*.

Most of the techniques described in this book are intended to create an altered state of consciousness that is closer to the dream state than the waking state. In this state, *tonal* and *nahual* merge, with help from breathing techniques or other practices. This state is not governed by physical or temporal laws, so can create changes that defy time and what we consider possible.

Seven Energy Centres

The ancient Mexicans had two names for the energy centres that are known in other traditions as chakras. Their equivalents for the word 'chakra' were *totonalcayo*, 'heat-producing spot', and *cuecueyo*, from the Náhuatl word *cuey*, 'curved'.

They also had two chakra systems. The first one came from the Chichimeca, Tolteca and Mexihca areas (the north and centre of Mexico) and the second one from the southern areas, near the Mayan region. The second one is much more similar to the traditional chakra system known worldwide.

I prefer to work with the first system, as I think it is more authentic. It is Mexican, it is listed in one of the pre-Columbian codices, and, as it includes ancestors, the calendar, flowers, dreams and flints, it reflects the ancient Mexican cosmology.

The second system is an adaptation of the Eastern chakra system, but with its own unique characteristics. I have included it here because some people use it, including Xolotl, one of my teachers, but I mainly use the first one in my courses and seminars around the world.

The First System

1. *Colotl,* 'scorpion'

Located at the coccyx, colour: black

It is said that the scorpion's tail made 'old winds' or energies come down, that is, it brought our ancestors' energy or energy from our own past lives into our current life. Many people know this as karma. This is why this centre is the only one located in our back, and the energy radiates in that direction, while the others radiate their energy to the front.

2. *Ihuitl,* 'feather'

Located in the genital area, colours: red and white

Sexual energy, *coatzin,* the venerable serpent, is in charge of creating whatever happens in our life, for good or ill. The feather metaphor is very similar to that used in the Egyptian Book of the Dead: the *coatzin* serpent needs to be as light as a feather so that it can rise upwards and so lighten our heavy emotions, prevent us from falling ill and help us free ourselves from our needs and instincts.

3. *Pantli*, 'flag'

Located in the belly button, colour: white

For the ancient Mexicans, the flag symbolized the number 20. There are 20 calendar glyphs, which relate to the five fingers on each hand and the five toes on each foot, which are 20 in total, hence the number 20 makes us a complete being. We are all born under one of the 20 calendar glyphs and a particular number. The combination is known as *tonalli* and is always drawn in a flag. For example, in my case it is 8 Lizard. Each *tonalli* has particular gifts and challenges. For example, an unbalanced 8 Lizard will be trapped in pleasure and sexuality, whereas a balanced 8 Lizard will be prolific in artistic and related activities and occult sciences. Healing this third energy centre helps us to transfer our energy from the painful aspects of our *tonalli* to the most favourable ones, even if we don't know what our *tonalli* is.

4. *Xochitl*, 'flower'

Located in the chest, colour: red

This centre is the place of union between past and future, precious knowledge and renewal, the sky's creative energy and the heavy energy of the underworlds. When the flower is blooming, all these energies are working together in harmony and generating beauty in our life. If this centre is not balanced, however, pain and sadness will be present instead.

5. *Topilli*, 'sceptre'

Located in the throat, colour: blue

This is the centre of personal power, triumphs, failures and the magic power of creation, which can be, according to the Náhuatl proverb, as beautiful as jade or turquoise or as destructive as a sharp-pointed obsidian. So this energy centre can be used to restore our personal power at all levels.

6. *Chalchiuhuitl*, 'jade'

Located on the forehead, colour: green

For the ancient Mexicans, jade was the most precious substance there was; it was even more precious than gold. Our emotions are located in the jade chakra and it is also the place where the *tonal* and *nahual*, the waking and sleeping states, consciousness and dreaming, meet. When we enter a state of 'dreaming while awake', using the techniques presented in this book, we can reach incredible goals.

7. *Tecpatl*, 'flint'

Located at the crown, colours: red and black

Flint represents reflection and justice – the justice that is meted out to us as a result of our actions, dreams and words. So we can use this centre to change our destiny from one of suffering to one of peace and even enlightenment.

The Second System

1. *Tlalli*, 'soil'

Located between the anus and the genitals, colours: black and red

It was believed that this centre was made from obsidian. Its colours are related to Mother Earth and the Cosmic Mother.

2. *Tleltl*, 'fire'

Located in the sexual area, colours: vary in tone, as does fire itself

This is the centre that governs sexual energy and its creations.

3. *Quiahuiztli*, 'rain'

Located in the solar plexus

Water is related to the emotions, which is why this is held to be the emotional centre.

4. *Ehecatl*, 'wind'

Located in the heart

This point is related to the four winds: the one that blesses, the one that purifies, the one that takes off thorns and the one that brings curses. It is also related to the *teyolia* energy body, hence the experiences of our lives and dreams, which in turn attract different circumstances to our lives.

5. *Nacatl tlaxtequi*, 'the thing that cuts meat'

Located in the throat

This refers to the positive and negative power of words, which can create or destroy lives – that is to say, cut the meat.

6. *Ixquihta Nahuatoton,* 'the eye in the sky'

Located where the third eye is commonly placed

This centre has clairvoyant and daydreaming properties.

7. *Xochiyotl,* 'the flower's essence'

Located at the crown

This centre can activate our blooming, or enlightenment.

There are many ways in which the energetic bodies and *totonalcayos* can be used to improve our lives. Some of them will be presented in this book. I will start by describing a basic way of balancing the energy centres with the power of sound.

EXERCISE: BALANCING THE *TOTONALCAYOS* WITH THE POWER OF SOUND

I suggest you do this exercise every morning before starting your daily routine and again at the end of the day.

~ In this exercise, you make the following sounds for a few seconds as if you were singing: 'Tzaaaaa', 'Tzeeeee', 'Tziiiii', 'Tzooooo' and 'Tzuuuuu'.

~ Each sound will balance one point, beginning with the lowest.

~ So, start with 'Tzaaaaa'. This will balance the first *totonalcayo* (in either system).

⌇ Then move to 'Tzeeeee', which will balance the second.

⌇ 'Tziiiii', 'Tzooooo' and 'Tzuuuuu' will balance the third, fourth and fifth.

⌇ Then start again with 'Tzaaaaa' to balance the sixth point, and so on.

⌇ Continue until you have balanced each of the *totonalcayos* three times, then end with 'Tziiiii' for all the energy points, making a fourth time. (*I will explain the significance of the number four in the following chapter.*)

⌇ Finally, put your hands together – the symbol of creation – and say:

> *Ometeotl* [o-may-tay-ot-l, meaning 'two energies brought together to create']. I state that all of my *totonalcayos* [to-ton-al-kai-os] are balanced with sound power. *Ometeotl.*

CHAPTER 2

Toltec Numerology

I have often heard the expression 'God must be a mathematician.' The ancient Mexicans, too, described primal energy, Centeotl, as 'the one who gives measure and movement'. Understanding creation therefore meant understanding numbers and their relation to us.

The mathematical order of the cosmos was also related directly to the body and the energetic system or *totonalcayos*. So it was used in healing, and in a variety of other ways too, including verbally. In Náhuatl, *tlahtolli* meant 'word' and *tlahtollin* meant 'the mathematical order of creation'.

The Meaning of Numbers

It is essential to understand at least what the numbers one to 20 meant for Teotihuacáns, Mayans, Aztecs and Toltecs, for several reasons. First, to understand the techniques that I will share with you and the number of times that you have to repeat them, and secondly to understand why some of the cycles are based on the numbers seven, nine and 13. Then you will understand why amazing healing results can come from the application of sacred mathematics. Such healing practices need time and space to work, but with them you can achieve a transformation. And you will realize that this form of healing is not magic, but an ancient reproducible science.

Here are the numbers from one to 20 and their meanings:

Ce: One, or Unit

We start with the abstract concept of the primal energy of all creation. The ancient Mexicans called it Centeotl, primal energy, creative energy or unity energy. Centeotl is the power before and beyond our mind and dreams, the power from which everything emanates.

In fact, when we refer to the number one, we are referring to primal energy *before* creation. That's why we can't perform any healing technique only once. The first time we do it, we are only expressing our intention, as it were, to primal energy – we are far from actually using it to manifest. It is by repeating our intentions that we express them in what is called matter.

The first *totonalcayo*, Colotl (scorpion), is related to this number, as Centeotl creates us using this *totonalcayo* as a starting point. So it is linked to the energy on which our entire existence is based and it expresses what the ancient Mexicans called the old winds and people now call karma.

Ome: Two

According to the ancient Mexicans, primal energy must divide in two to start creating. In the Toltec tradition these two creative forces are represented by a man and a woman, Ometecuhtli and Omecihuatl, Mr Two and Mrs Two, who create through the power of sound and smoke. In the Mexican codices they are depicted as a man blowing a *caracol*, a conch that is blown in ceremonies, and a woman smudging. They are equivalent to the Oriental concept of yin and yang.

The Náhuatl word *ometeotl*, 'two forces that unite to create', has its roots here. We use this word whenever we open a ceremony or healing session in order to set our intention. Afterwards, we close our ceremony with the same word. You will have used it already when balancing your *totonalcayos* with sound in the previous exercise.

The word for 'two', *ome*, comes from the Omilt root word for 'bone'. In a bamboo stem, two parts unite to create a hollow cylinder. Bones, too, are hollow cylinders. For the ancient Mexicans, bones and stones recorded the past. Bones and blood were the equivalent of modern DNA, the place where ancestral memories and hidden codes were stored. The energy of our ancestors and our own past lay in our bones.

This is related to the second *totonalcayo*, Ihuitl (feather), because our creations, whether they are 'heavy' or 'light', will repeat the patterns of our ancestors until we become aware of this and do something to overcome the invisible prison of our inheritance. Memories may have to be erased from our bones through a variety of techniques if we are determined to make substantial changes to our life.

Although the two energies are creating, they are still far from manifesting. For this reason, to be successful, healing and rejuvenation techniques must be performed more than twice.

Yei: Three

This comes from the word *yeztli*, 'blood'. There are two different approaches to understanding the concept of blood: human blood, which I will talk about later on, and the energy produced when the two forces of creation, Ometecuhtli and Omecihuatl, are united. In modern terminology, these two represent the electric and the magnetic forces, and together they start generating a new energy, a new creation. So two become three.

The ancient Mexicans depicted this process as blood flowing through a hollow bone – new energy that is a combination of the two previous energies but has not yet become either matter or life. Therefore, it is not enough to repeat a technique three times.

As for human blood, it is sacred and from the ancient perspective it brings together the two creative principles of human beings: *tonal* and *nahual*, the being we are in the waking state and the being we are in the sleep state.

Why is it that blood brings these two together? It is stated that when we are in the womb, we are using our *nahual*, our energetic body, to dream of who we were and who we will become. When we are born, covered in blood, we make contact for the first time with our *tonal*, our waking self, and our blood remembers the contact between *tonal* and *nahual* and remains a bridge between them, between our waking and sleeping selves.

All our experiences in both the *nahual* and the *tonal* are recorded in our blood. As it flows through our body, so does the vibration of our past, including our ancestral past. Blood is related to the third *totonalcayo*, Pantli (flag), because we were born into a certain family, a certain bloodline, on a certain day, and the ancient Mexicans showed this by a calendar glyph and a number that were always drawn in a flag. So the flag is the symbol of both our blood inheritance and the influence of our horoscope on our life.

In this book I will teach you how to activate the power of your blood. This is one of the greatest powers inside you, your own hidden medicine.

Nahui: Four

Nahui comes from *nantli*, 'mother', and *hui*, 'order' – the order of the Cosmic Mother and Mother Earth, in the sense of a mother giving life. How does this happen? One, which represents thought, divides into two, the creative forces Ometecuhtli and Omecihuatl, which transform themselves into what we call Father Thought and Mother Thought, and combine to create four forces that are the pillars of everything that exists.

The ancient Mexicans were aware that the foundations of life and each of its cycles were based on the number four, and that four elements from the Earth were required to create life. Now science has confirmed the fact that four elements are required for life. You can find this mathematical order in everything that exists as well as in the cycles of nature, such as four elements and four seasons, and two solstices and two equinoxes completing a solar cycle.

For this reason, doing the practices I will teach in this book four times is the minimum required to get results. This will link with other mathematical cycles too. If the practice has an affinity with the number nine, for example, doing it four times will make 36 (9 × 4) in total. If the practice has an affinity with the number 13, doing it four times will make 52 (13 × 4), which is related to the cycle of the Pleiades and Orion, as we will see later on. Numbers and the universe are directly related to each other, and by carrying out the practices four times, you will always be aligned with the mother's order and giving life to something new.

You also need to share your thoughts and dreams with Mother Earth so they can manifest. This is related to the fourth *totonalcayo*, Xochitl (flower), because the word used for manifesting in ancient Mexico was 'flowering', meaning that the four forces and the Earth allowed it to exist.

Later I will describe how to hand your creations to Tonantzin, our venerable Mother Earth, so that she can bring them to life.

Mahcuilli: Five

Mahcuilli means 'to grip something with the fingers' and, in a deeper sense, 'the worms in the hands', meaning our fingers. The fact that each of our hands has five fingers shows the enormous power of the number five to create.

Whatever plans we have shared with Mother Earth in our dreams and thoughts will be carried out by means of our fingers. This is related to the fifth *totonalcayo*, Topilli (sceptre), because our hands give us the power to do many things. Metaphorically, they are the power of creation.

The fact that our fingers are made of bones, which contain information about our ancestors, can prevent us from achieving our goals, though, because it is tough to manifest something different from what our ancestors have gone through. Therefore, in order to create something new, it is essential to heal your ancestors and rid yourself of their negative patterns.

Chicoacen: Six

Chicoacen means 'the power of the serpent united' or 'the power of energy unified'. As a principle, six is the energy of our bones and ancestors, the creative power of our blood, the Earth's capacity to give life and our own ability to carry out actions in our day-to-day lives, all expressed through our energy bodies (*see page 3*) and energy centres, or *totonalcayos* (*see pages 5–10*). It is through these bodies and centres that our inner self communicates with the outside world – the world that seems external but has been generated inside us.

The number six is also related to the sixth *totonalcayo*, Chalchiuhuitl (jade), because the energy we express through our unified system is our jade, our most precious gemstone, the energy that gives us the power to express ourselves through the way we live our life, and to change it if we wish.

Chicome: Seven

For the ancient Mexicans, the number seven represented creation, and it was strictly related to renewal, life and death and the power of the word. It symbolized the *tlahtolli*, 'word' or 'order', the system in which life is created by primal energy through the duality of bone and blood and expressed on Earth openly through what we do and energetically through our *totonalcayos*.

Seven is related to our seventh *totonalcayo*, Tecpatl (flint), because it represents the justice of what we are creating – the idea that we will reap what we sow.

In the ancient codices this idea was depicted as the cave of Chicomoztoc (*see page 33*), which was a way of expressing in pictographic form that our inner self is the origin of our outer world. That is why many of the techniques in this book will be based on the number seven.

If we multiply seven by four, the mother's order, we get 28, the moon cycle. So seven allows us to align ourselves with the moon, which, according to the ancient Mexicans, can bring us either fortune or disgrace. The moon is one of the most powerful forces of creation and destruction there is. By mere observation, we can see that the new moon represents a lack whereas the full moon represents an excess. And as one of the moon's faces is dark while the other is bright, when we align our practices with the moon's cycles, we get striking results.

Chicuey: Eight

Chicuey is 'the power of the bloodstream', and this bloodstream refers to the energy of the universe. We are considering the universe at this point because eight is the number where we jump from the personal to the collective. It is here that the dreams we are generating within through the seven previous numbers integrate with the dreams being created by others. Many connections with other beings are woven through the invisible web of dreams.

This takes place in our inner world, our cave, and thus it is our inner self that determines what the universe brings to us. People may cross our path in a seemingly random way and situations come out of nowhere, but it is all secretly synchronized from within.

We may not be aware of what we are creating, however. Eight is related to darkness, to night, and therefore to what is not clear. It has to do with what is hidden in our unconscious, in our cave. Therapeutically, it is associated with all the things that are buried deep in the darkness of our own shadow, waiting to be processed and causing us trouble in the meantime.

It is also associated with what the ancient Mexicans called 'illumination through the path of darkness', in other words, exploring our dreams and our instincts, as well as altered states of consciousness, and becoming the lord or lady of our cave, that is, mastering our inner self and being able to express it outwardly in our life.

Chicnahui: Nine

Nine is also associated with what is hidden, but, unlike eight, it refers to what is hidden within the Earth. The ancient Mexicans envisioned what they called underworlds as places where your mind could be trapped by recurrent patterns, limiting paradigms or destructive emotions that were repeated again and again in your dreams and consequently also in your life.

However, nine is the number that brings all your problems to the surface so that you can overcome them. For this reason, it is widely used in healing practices. It connects with what is hidden inside you, in the Earth, in the underworlds, in your own darkness, so that you can heal yourself and others.

Nine also 'centres' eight to prevent it from creating uncontrolled events. Those who can work with the number nine to overcome their problems will access the caves of power where the word 'impossible' does not exist, and will assume control over their life.

Mahtlactli: 10

Mahtlactli not only means 10 but also, in a deeper sense, the back of the hand. This emphasizes the fact that you can do a lot with a hand with five fingers, but when you add a second hand you get 10 fingers and can therefore do far more.

Two hands also enable you to modify what you have been doing up to now. This is why 10 can simply mean change – changing what you were used to doing for a new way of doing things. That is why many of the healing techniques presented here have an affinity with the number 10. Therapeutically, it is widely used to promote discipline, heal emotions and change previous patterns. Through using it, you can embrace the future and even develop prophetic powers.

Mahtlactli Once (10 plus One): 11

A new cycle starts here, a new set of five, which will result, metaphorically, in the toes of a foot. The feet symbolize the path you walk along, and as what you have been doing has now changed, the direction you are moving in should also change. If you are expressing the potential of the number 11 in your life, it means that you are walking a new path.

This is not always pleasant, though. If you are resistant to change, 11 can bring about diseases, crises or breakdowns that will force you to change. Our planet is going through this now. Some big crises are forcing us to change our course.

Since most of the time 11 produces change through a lot of suffering, it is not used in healing.

Mahtlactli Omome (10 plus Two): 12

We have come a long way from one to 10. Changing what we were doing forced us to change the direction we were going in. Now we are entering new territory.

I would like to explain here that most people cannot reach these numerological levels. They remain trapped in their underworld, unable to change what they do. They are trapped by nine and can never access 10, though doing so is very simple. All it takes is changing what you do, though this simple act can lead to complexity, because it leads to changing direction and changing your character. That will take you to number 12, the number of wisdom. This refers to the wisdom you have gained along the way: the ability to recognize your past without repeating it, so that all that you have experienced will now fill your new path with wisdom.

Mahtlactli Oneyi (10 plus Three): 13

According to ancient Mexican numerology, 13 is one of the most important numbers, or even *the* most important number. It refers to the 13 heavens – the 13 steps required by primal energy to become matter. It is also directly related to the sun. The ancient Mexicans were perfectly aware of the fact that the rotation of the solar equator takes 26 terrestrial days, meaning that the sun shows a different face to us every 13 days. This 13-day period is commonly known in Mexico as a *trecena*, a 13-day period, which is, in fact, a solar wave. This explains why the Mayans, Toltecs and Aztecs divided their calendars into 13-day cycles.

The sun was the archetype of enlightenment for many ancient cultures, so the number 13 had this connotation too. Enlightenment involves, among other things, healing your ancestors, transforming yourself and freeing yourself from your underworlds so that you can gain access to precious knowledge. Quetzalcóatl, the lord of light and knowledge, was the archetype of enlightenment for the ancient Mexicans (Kukulcan was for the Mayans), so 13 is associated with him too.

In healing, 13 is constantly used to gain access to the most refined knowledge about the universe. It is also used to ensure that something manifests in the most beautiful way.

Mahtlactli Onnahui (10 plus Four): 14

Fourteen is a new beginning after the 13-day period, the *trecena*, and enlightenment or blossoming. It is a resumption of the count. Naturally, since we have blossomed, the path we are walking now is perfectly synchronized with both the cosmic and the terrestrial order.

Often we use both our hands in rituals and healing practices with the purpose of establishing a new order in our life and after a *trecena* in terms of time. That is why in the healing and manifestation techniques presented here, the 14th step is often shown by putting your hands together and saying '*Ometeotl*' along with the command for whatever you want to bring into existence.

Caxtolli: 15

This number completes the third cycle of five, the first foot. The term for it has its roots in 'knowledge of the movement of the celestial gourd shell container', in other words, the cycles of the universe.

It is with the number 15 that the Toltec path starts. Why? *Caxtolli* literally means 'the one who understands the measure'. What measure? The cosmic measure, from thousands of years to minor lunar cycles and the different movements of each day.

Caxtolli Once (15 plus One): 16

A new five-day cycle starts here. In the numerology of the human body, it marks the beginning of the last foot. At this point you are walking in alignment with the cosmic order.

In the human realm, this means not only mastering the cycles of the universe but using them to create. Many of the healing and manifestation techniques that I will present in this book use the mathematics of the universe for this purpose.

Caxtolli Omome (15 plus Two): 17

Here you can see how far you've come, because 17 brings duality back, as it is *caxtolli omome*, 15 plus two. This means that you have mastered the duality of the waking world and the dreaming world and are able to merge them in order to produce the changes that some people call miracles but really are just the ability to make two worlds one, because they are one.

Caxtolli Oneyi (15 plus Three): 18

As you will remember, three is related to blood. Fifteen plus three stands for the person who has been awakened by the power of the serpent, in other words by its energy and wisdom, by all the power in its blood. Because of this, they can interact with the blood of the universe, with its energy, at will.

In this book you will find techniques designed to awaken the sacred power of your blood, to honour it and to use it for healing and manifestation.

Caxtolli Onnahui (15 plus Four): 19

Four is associated with the order of the mother, and since 15 is related to the celestial gourd shell container, 19 isn't linked to Mother Earth but the Cosmic Mother. It represents the one who can visit the Cosmic Mother.

A way to visit her is not to lose consciousness when you sleep in complete darkness, but to stay in a lucid dream instead. That way, you will stay in the Cosmic Mother, that is, in a kind of meditation while you are asleep. If you can do this, you will have incredible powers when you wake up. If you can reach level 19 in the Toltec tradition, you will clearly realize that you can influence what people call reality.

You will also have overcome the hidden force that has been ruling you: your unconscious.

Cempohualli: 20

Twenty represents being full of experience – experience that allows you to be empty. So you are also full of emptiness. It is the number that ends the fourth five-day cycle and marks the completion of the second foot, enabling you to walk any path you want.

Now the count goes back again and starts from one – not from zero, but from a position of being full of knowledge and happy to start a different movement, a different cycle.

A sculpture that shows this numerical system is the one of Coatlicue, the divine mother, goddess of fertility and ruler of life and death, that can be seen in the National Museum of Anthropology in Mexico City. She is depicted as a woman wearing a skirt of snakes and a necklace of human hearts.

Coatlicue

For the ancient Mexicans, 'death' referred not only to physical death, but also to major change. When observing this figure, you can see that she has both her hands and feet as well as her skull in the centre of the image. In other words, to make changes, heal or perform what some people call miracles, as well as, of course, to prepare for our next great change, dying consciously and lucidly, we need to follow these 20 steps. The hands represent our actions, which will determine the path our feet will walk.

In this book you will find many practical tools to align yourself with the universe and use cosmic cycles and numerology for healing, manifestation and rejuvenation. Ultimately, you will be able to awaken the power of your blood and be at one with the universe.

Ometeotl.

CHAPTER 3

The Caves of Power

Though I first started learning about healing when I was a child, curiously enough it was what I learned last that proved the most important. It boosted the effectiveness of my therapies to a remarkable degree. So far, there has been no written record of this hermetic knowledge.

Despite the fact that these ancient techniques came into my life last, they will be the first I will include here, so, unlike me, you don't have to wait 20 years or more to receive these secret instructions.

This body of knowledge is known as 'the caves of power', a reference to the power hidden in the inner self. For the ancient Mexicans, the inner self was the part of ourselves where our dreams and underworlds resided. Our instincts and unconscious were also there. So, our power is hidden in the darkness of our cave. If activated, it will enable us to have almost total control over our life.

In all, there are 20 caves of power, 20 ways of working with our inner self. Seven correspond to a series of actions we can carry out in the *tonal*, the waking state, for self-empowerment. The other 13 correspond to actions we can only carry out in the *nahual*, the dream state. Since this book is mainly devoted to healing and not to dreams, I will only describe the seven practices we can perform while we are awake. I aim to cover the rest in future books. However, those of us who have been fortunate enough to receive this knowledge have been carefully trained in these practices and covering only the first seven caves here means that you too will receive this training gradually and correctly.

The Place of the Seven Caves

One of the stories in the chronicles of the foundation of Tenochtitlan (today Mexico City) relates that in ancient times the Aztecs lived in Aztlan. This is depicted as a place full of herons, where all the houses were white, the people were kind and Náhuatl was the language. Nevertheless, seven different tribal groups migrated from Aztlan on a pilgrimage to find the promised land. They would know they had found it when they saw an eagle perched on a cactus devouring a serpent.

My attention is drawn here to the similarity between the words 'Aztlan' and 'Atlantis'. There may be a connection, but this is mere personal conjecture. Some academics consider that Aztlan was real, others think it was mythical. The word 'Aztec' does, however, come from Aztlan: the Aztecs are 'those who came from Aztlan'.

The chronicles relate that during their pilgrimage the seven tribal groups of Aztlan lived for a while in a cave called

Chicomoztoc

Chicomoztoc. This is literally, according to academics, 'the place of the seven caves'. So investigators are out there looking for real caves. Mystics are even looking for portals to other dimensions. Some say Chicomoztoc was located in Guanajuato, others in El Cerro de la Estrella and others in the pyramids of Teotihuacán. But to me and many others who follow the Mexihca and Toltec tradition, the codex is pretty clear. It describes a fantastic inner world that is connected to the outer world through seven portals that take you from the inside to the outside, from the *nahual* to the *tonal*, from your unconscious to your everyday life. It refers to the seven caves of power – the seven *totonalcayos*, or chakras.

The Seven Caves

To activate the Chicomoztoc, the seven caves, means to connect our inner power to what we call reality, so we can express this power in the form of healing, rejuvenation and manifestation.

Before we can do this, we need to enter the darkness to recover our creative power. In our tradition, darkness is not something evil – that is simply a modern prejudice. The view of the ancient people of Mexico was the same as that written in the Bible: light shines out of darkness. That is, darkness will give life to our creations.

In ancient times, these practices were for a select group only and were performed in the darkness of physical caves, but they can be performed equally well outside caves.

The First Cave: *Tonal*

The first cave is called Tonal, meaning 'day' and 'who you are when you are awake', which can be interpreted as who your mind thinks you are – your personality.

There are many caves in Mexico that have a hole in the top. Academics think they were ancient observatories, but this is just part of the truth, because they were also used in the spiritual training of priests, warriors, rulers and practitioners of nahualism, the art of dreaming. Many of the practices I will describe here were done in this type of cave and we do them there to this day.

Ideally, this first exercise should carried out in such a cave, but if it is not possible, you could also do it in a dark place with light filtering through. Stay there as long as possible to see how the light filters through the darkness, because this will leave you with an unconscious imprint of how creation takes place. In the Mexican tradition, the primal energy of creation, Centeotl, is also known as Black Eagle, or Amomati, the state without mind.

Exercise: Illuminating Your Darkness – Healing Your Inner Self

This core exercise is done to balance and heal yourself, not others. It consists of taking the light filtering through the hole at the top of the cave and introducing it into your seven *totonalcayos*, while asking it to give you the power to balance them all inside yourself and in others. Start at the crown. (*I am using the first system here.*)

- *Tecpatl* (flint), crown: Ask the light filtering down into the cave to change the justice you are receiving and endow you with healing powers. Here you are asking to heal the old winds, the karmic patterns, in your life and create something better.

- *Chalchiuhuitl* (jade), forehead: Ask the light to give you the ability to enter an altered state through the merging of your *nahual* [na-wal] and *tonal* [tone-al]. You will be able to use this state for healing, rejuvenation and manifestation for both yourself and your patients (if you have any).

∼ *Topilli* (sceptre), throat: Take the light to your throat and ask it to awaken your personal power.

∼ *Xochitl* (flower), chest: Take the light to your chest and ask for the power to heal your ancestors and your underworlds, to align yourself with the precious knowledge, to create from the heavens and to change what we consider to be real.

∼ *Pantli* (flag), navel: Take the light to your navel and ask it to allow you to express your horoscope in the most favourable way and to enable you to use your gifts for the benefit of others.

∼ *Ihuitl* (feather), genital area: Take the light to your genitals and ask it to change the creation of hardships and diseases in your life and the lives of others to the creation of something better.

∼ *Colotl* (scorpion), coccyx: Take the light to your coccyx with the purpose of healing not only your own ancestral patterns but also those of others.

You need to do this process at least four times.

I would like to add that the more power you want to get, the more often you need to carry out this process. I have done it 28 times in a cave very close to Teotihuacán, and I plan to keep doing it in the future.

The Second Cave: *Mahcuilmetztli*

In my opinion, the second cave is one of the most important for healers, because it empowers the hands. The ancient Mexicans always took the relationship between the physical body and the cosmos into consideration in their healing practices. Bearing in mind that 'Mexico' means 'the place of the moon's navel', the relationship between the hand and the lunar cycle could not be ignored. So this cave is known as Mahcuilmetztli, 'the five moons', as there are five lunar phases and we have five fingers on each hand. These relate to one another as follows:

- *The Dark of the Moon:* This takes place one day before the new moon. It is the most important phase of the moon because it takes you back to the state of nothingness, Centeotl, Black Eagle, in order to create. It is symbolized by the thumb.

- *Waxing Moon:* This phase enables you to nurture what you have created so that eventually it can blossom – manifest in a beautiful way. In other words, it allows you to grow anything you want in your life and the lives of your clients and the other people you help. It is symbolized by the index finger.

- *Full Moon:* This phase provides you with maximum intensity so that all that you have created in the earlier phases can blossom. Obviously it is symbolized by the longest finger on the hand, the middle finger.

- *Waning Moon:* This phase allows you to reduce what you have created but do not want anymore, to destroy problems that could escalate (from aches to diseases for example) and to remove problematical emotions from your life and those of your clients. It is symbolized by the ring finger.

~ *New Moon:* This phase is a time for starting new cycles and is symbolized by the little finger.

EXERCISE: SUMMONING THE POWER OF THE MOON

To truly have the power of the moon in your hands, you need to summon it and ask it to support you. Go outside during each of the five moon phases and use the corresponding finger to summon the power of the moon:

~ At the dark of the moon, summon the power of the dark moon to your thumb by pointing your thumb upwards and saying, 'Xihualhui [chi-wal-wee],' which means 'come' in Náhuatl, for nine minutes. Ask it to allow you to create whatever you wish.

~ When the moon enters the waxing phase, do the same, only this time using your index finger and asking for the power to make your creations grow.

~ On a full moon, do the same with your middle finger, evoking the power of the full moon to make your requests and healings blossom.

- On the waning moon, repeat the process with your ring finger, asking the moon to enable you to reduce your problems and, if appropriate, your patients' problems.

- Finally, at the new moon, repeat the process with your little finger, this time asking the moon to create new cycles in your life and your patients' lives.

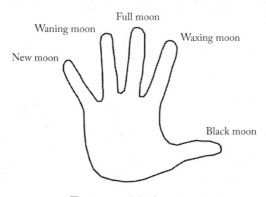

The moon and the fingers

Remember, the more you practise, the more you'll be able to use the power of the moon. Also remember that according to the ancient Mexicans, the moon can bring you fortune or disgrace.

The Third Cave: *Tlahtlani*

The third cave, Tlahtlani, 'questioning', is an absolutely fascinating one.

EXERCISE: QUESTIONING

In ancient times people performed this exercise in a physical cave to ask themselves why they were following the path of nahualism. Nowadays, it doesn't matter where you are, you can visit your inner cave at any time just by questioning yourself.

- Ask, 'Who am I? What am I doing here? Why am I learning all of this? Why do I want to become a healer?' and so on. This may bring great answers to you.

- As a rule, before giving any form of therapy, you should go to your cave and ask, 'Why am I doing this?'

I have had almost every possible answer to this last question, ranging from 'Because I love this person' to 'Because I want a better world', 'Because I want to demonstrate my power to myself' and, many times, 'Because I need to make a living.' Getting that answer is vital, because it shows you have the most wonderful thing: honesty.

Of course, you cannot reveal these answers. They are for you alone.

The Fourth Cave: *Mahuiltihtinemi*

The fourth cave is extremely meaningful because not only does it empower you immensely but it also allows you to make significant changes to your personality. It is called Mahuiltihtinemi, 'the cave of the game'. Etymologically, this means 'pleasure'!

Why is this important? It's because it's the energy that gives you pleasure that you use for healing. For example, if food, sex or television gives you pleasure, you will use that energy to heal.

EXERCISE: TURNING PLEASURE INTO POWER

~ Put your hands together in the shape of a bowl in front of your Ihuitl energy centre in your sexual area.

~ Call the pleasure that certain actions, for example eating, bring you to come to your hands by saying 'Xihualhui.'

~ When you feel the energy arriving, just lift your hands towards your throat, to the Topilli energy centre in your neck, and command that the pleasure you are holding transforms into healing power.

~ Then put both hands together and say: 'Ometeotl.'

I recommend practising this exercise on a daily basis to transform pleasure into the power to heal yourself and others. You can also use it to overcome addictions.

The Fifth Cave: *Cemi*

'The cave of the feather of altered consciousness' is the one that allows you to enter (or, as the ancients termed it, drink) the state of dreaming while awake. This is an altered state of consciousness that allows you to alter reality just as you can in lucid dreams.

You enter this state by merging the *tonal* and *nahual*. There are many ways to ask for the power to do this. I will give you a very simple one that can be done anywhere.

EXERCISE: YOUR FEATHER

This should take place on the day of the new moon.

~ Write a message to the moon asking her to bring you a feather for dreaming while awake.

~ Now burn your request and blow the ashes to the moon.

~ The next feather that you find or that someone gives you as a present will be from the bird that will become your ally and help you reach this altered state of consciousness.

You can do this exercise many times and if you collect many feathers, your ability to dream while awake will increase.

One of my teachers once told me that if you received the feather of a vulture or any other scavenger bird in this exercise, it would be much more powerful than that of any other bird. I remember thinking, *That would be difficult, because who would give you a vulture's feather? And you'd be even more unlikely to just find one.*

However, life gave me a great lesson. A month after I had made my request, a woman who was taking one of my courses in Italy approached me and said, 'Look! I have a present for you. I got it from a place of power.' It was seven vulture feathers. I couldn't believe it. These feathers give the power to transform beyond death.

However, if you get a feather from any other bird, that will be perfect too. Whatever it is, the bird will empower you with its qualities. However, *you must either find or be given your feather. It is forbidden to buy it.*

You should keep your feather in the place where you do your healing. Ideally, you should keep two feathers from the same species or two from two different species. That will help you to take your patients into the deepest altered state of consciousness.

The Sixth Cave: *Yohulapa*

The sixth cave of power is my favourite. It is called Yohulapa, which comes from the words for 'night', 'darkness' and 'immensity'.

We have already mentioned that light comes from darkness, which is the deepest part of us and the most powerful force as well. In the sixth cave, you have to make an alliance with darkness in order to heal: you have to embrace the night.

EXERCISE: EMBRACING THE NIGHT

You can do this wherever you happen to be – in a field, in a cave, in your garden – as long as you do it in the dark of night.

~ It consists of tiptoeing for at least 18 minutes through the darkness, as quietly as you can, so that you enter a kind of trance.

~ Then surrender to the night, asking it to give you the power of healing others from the deep darkness of their inner selves. Ask it to empower you so that you can bring light from darkness for yourself and for others.

~ Once you have done this enough times, you will suddenly feel something putting its arms around you. It is the night, the darkness, the unconscious, the Cosmic Mother, making friends with you.

The Seventh Cave: *Onolhui*

The seventh cave of power is called Onolhui. It means 'moving energy in the direction you want it to go'.

I won't give you an exercise to perform here because all the techniques that I present in this book consist of moving energy in the direction you want it to go. This concept is known as *Teomanía* and is based on the sacred mathematics that direct movement. It is the subject of the next chapter.

So, these are the first seven caves of power. The other 13 can only be accessed in lucid dreams or altered states of consciousness. I look forward to writing about them in the future.

If you practise the exercises I have given here, I am positive that you will get amazing results and will benefit from the secrets of ancient Mexico that are being revealed now.

Welcome to the caves of power, the power of your inner self.

CHAPTER 4

Teomanía: Breathing Exercises

If you look up *Teomanía* in a Spanish or Náhuatl dictionary, you'll find it translated as 'meditation'. However, this is a mistranslation, because it actually means 'to move energy harmoniously with the universe and its cycles to obtain results'. This is done through breathing exercises according to the mathematics of the universe.

Although there are several types of *Teomanía*, the form I will describe here can be used as a complete exercise for personal self-healing. Many of my students all over the world have abandoned their former spiritual practices in favour of mathematical exercises such as this one.

It can also be used as an introduction to many different types of therapy. If used in this way, it consists of alternating a breathing cycle, or 'movement', with one of the healing exercises I give in this book.

As you now know, the ancient Mexicans observed that the basis of all change was the number four; so the shortest form of *Teomanía* consists of four movements.

Teomanía in Four Movements

Before starting, we need to review the meaning of some numbers:

- *Thirteen* is the number of the changing face of the sun, hence transformation, healing and ultimately blooming.

- *Eight* is the number of what is hidden or trapped in the unconscious and is generating all kinds of problems.

So, working in line with the cosmic order and its sacred mathematics, the process consists of inhaling through your nose, at your own pace, while mentally counting up to 13, to absorb the healing and transformative power of the sun, then exhaling through your mouth, again at your own pace, while mentally counting up to eight, to expel the unconscious or hidden energy that is creating your problems.

Inhaling to a count of 13 and exhaling to a count of eight is one breathing cycle. Thirteen breathing cycles are one movement. Four movements are 52 breaths. Now, 52 is an extremely important number, since every 52 years the three stars of Orion's Belt form a perfectly perpendicular line, as seen from the Earth, and the constellation of the Pleiades returns to the same position in the cosmos. For the ancient people, this meant the start of a new cycle, which was marked by a 'new fire' celebration. Hence when you perform 52 breathing cycles every day, you start transforming until you reach your new fire – a new way of dreaming that will be reflected in a new way of living.

EXERCISE: *TEOMANÍA* IN FOUR MOVEMENTS

This should ideally be performed in the morning. It can be done sitting or lying down, though sitting is preferable, either in the lotus position or simply in a chair, facing east, which is the sun's direction.

FIRST MOVEMENT

'~ Close your eyes and, counting to 13, inhale through your nose the healing and transformative power of the sun.

'~ Now, counting to eight, exhale through your mouth all the energy hidden in your cave that is causing you problems.

'~ Repeat this process 12 times, making 13 times in total. A simple way to count the number of breaths is with the help of your fingers.

'~ When you have finished, pause briefly and then say, either verbally or mentally:

Ce ollin [say olin], first movement.

'~ It is in this first movement that you place the creative force of your intentions into Centeotl's mind. So now express your intention by saying, for example:

I dedicate this first movement to establishing the intention of healing my emotions and my relationships.

~ Be concrete and specific about what you want to heal. To reinforce the effectiveness of this practice, you can visualize what you desire.

SECOND MOVEMENT

Once you have finished, start doing the second movement in the same way:

~ Counting to 13, inhale through your nose the healing and transformative power of the sun.

~ Counting to eight, exhale through your mouth all the energy of your ancestors that is causing your troubles.

~ Do this process 13 times.

~ When you have finished, pause briefly and then say:

> *Ome ollin* [o-may olin], second movement. May the energy of the universe come down in the form of a snake.

~ Visualize a serpent, the ancestral symbol of healing, descending through your crown and travelling through your body, erasing all the suffering of your ancestors as well as the energy imprinted in your bones that was causing these problems. Wait until you feel you have finished the task.

~ Once you have finished, stamp with your right foot on Mother Earth and ask her to absorb this energy.

~ Stamp once again, this time asking Mother Earth to do something beautiful with this energy.

THIRD MOVEMENT

Immediately afterwards, start doing the third movement, carrying out the same process:

~ Counting to 13, inhale the healing power of the sun.

~ Counting to eight, exhale all the negative emotions trapped in your organs, as well as all the damage that might exist in them.

~ Do this process 13 times.

~ Once you have finished, pause briefly and say:

> *Yei ollin* [jay olin], third movement.

~ Let me remind you that *yei* comes from the word *yeztli*, which means 'blood'. So now give the command:

> May the healing power of my blood awaken. May my blood become my medicine.

~ Visualize the energy in your bloodstream passing through all your organs, particularly any that are damaged, healing them, repairing them and rejuvenating them. Continue until you feel the process has finished.

FOURTH MOVEMENT

~ Counting to 13, inhale the healing power of the sun.

~ Counting to eight, exhale your unconscious dreams and heavy creations.

~ Repeat this process 13 times.

∾ When you have finished, say:

> *Nahui ollin* [na-we olin], fourth movement. May I harmonize with Mother Earth. May she assist me in making changes.

∾ The following symbol represents the four movements. Draw this symbol on the Earth with your right index finger (in this tradition, the right hand is the one that projects; the left hand is the one that receives). The Earth will receive your intention and later it will manifest.

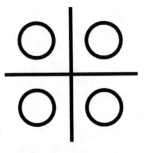

The four movements

∾ When you have finished, put your hands together, say '*Ometeotl* [o-may-tay-ot-l]' and then state all your intentions.

∾ Wait for a while until you feel the energy has moved, fulfilling your purpose. Then once again say '*Ometeotl*.'

In four movements, you have now completed the 52 cycle and reached the new fire, based on the mathematics of the Pleiades and Orion. New fire means new dreams, and if you have a new dream, your whole life will change.

Teomanía in four movements should be performed for 52 days in a row as a personal exercise. Optionally, as mentioned earlier, it can be used in conjunction with the other healing practices that I will outline in this book. Just alternate the movements with the healing practices.

If you want to make more substantial changes, you can continue your practice with *Teomanía* in eight movements.

EXERCISE: *TEOMANÍA* IN EIGHT MOVEMENTS

Complete the four movements from the previous exercise.

FIFTH MOVEMENT
Remember that *mahcuilli*, five, means gripping with the fingers.

~ Inhale through your nose, counting to 13, and exhale through your mouth, counting to eight, as before, for a cycle of 13 breaths. From now on, inhale the healing power of the sun each time and exhale the hidden causes of the specific problems you want to resolve.

~ Once you have finished, say:

> *Mahcuilli ollin* [ma-cwilli olin], fifth movement.

~ Think about all that you asked of Mother Earth in the fourth movement and point to the Earth with the tips of your fingers, keeping the palms of your hands facing the Earth as you ask, either mentally or out loud:

> May I receive the energy of the Earth through my fingers
> – all her healing power and her strength.

~ Feel the power of Mother Earth reaching you through your fingers.

~ Once you feel you have received enough energy from the Earth to make all the changes you want in your life, move on to the next movement.

SIXTH MOVEMENT

~ Do the breathing cycle another 13 times.

~ Give the command for the sixth movement:

Chicoacen ollin [chicwassen olin], sixth movement.

~ Point to the Earth once again with the palms of your hands facing the Earth and ask once again for the energy of Mother Earth to reach your fingertips.

~ Keep the palm of your left hand, the one that receives, pointing to the Earth and when you feel the energy of Mother Earth has reached you, put your right hand, the one that projects, on your sacrum, so that it projects the energy from the Earth.

~ Order this energy to go up to your sacrum, your genitals, your navel, your chest, your throat, your forehead and your crown, as if it were a twisting serpent.

~ Allow the serpent to come out through your head and keep going until it reaches the cosmos. In this way, you are uniting the energy of the Earth with that of the cosmos to create new life inside yourself.

~ Once you have finished, move on to the seventh movement.

SEVENTH MOVEMENT

Remember that *chicome*, seven, represents creation. *Chicome* means 'the power of the two energies united', referring to life being created through the bone and blood duality. Hence it is the most powerful number of creation.

~ Repeat the breathing cycle 13 times. Remember to inhale the healing power of the sun and exhale all the hidden factors that are causing trouble.

~ Once you have finished, choose two things that you would like to create, and direct all the power of the seventh movement to them with the words:

Chicome ollin [chico-me olin], seventh movement.

~ Once again with the palms of your hands facing Mother Earth, absorb all the energy you require. As you feel it, think about the first thing you wish to create, for example a job. Put your hands together, which, you will remember, is the symbol of creation, and say:

Ometeotl. May I get the job I desire. *Ometeotl.*

~ Separate your hands and again with the palms of your hands facing Mother Earth, ask for her energy.

~ Then repeat this with the second thing you want to create.

You are directing the power of the seventh movement towards your purposes.

~ If you see that as time passes by you are realizing your objectives, you may substitute new ones for them.

~ When you have finished, move on to the last movement.

EIGHTH MOVEMENT

~ Once again inhale, to a count of 13, the healing power of the sun and the force of change.

~ Exhale to a count of eight and ask to be free of all your inner problems as well as your outer problems.

~ Do this process 13 times.

~ When you have finished, give the command for the eighth movement:

> *Chicuey ollin* [chic-way olín], eighth movement. May all the right things come into my life in harmony with the flow of the energy of the universe, and may they come from all directions and my inner self.

~ Then put your hands together and give the final command:

> *Ometeotl.* May my ancestors, my family and my blood heal. May the Earth give me her energy. May the universe and the Earth be united through me. May what I desire manifest. *Ometeotl.*

~ Allow this energy to flow and you will have completed the *Teomanía* in eight movements.

When you have completed the eighth movement, you will have performed 104 breathing cycles. According to the ancient people, it takes the cosmos 104 years to return to the same position (as seen from an observation point on Earth), after which a new cosmic cycle starts. So, if you are going to complete the full eight movements, you would ideally do so 104 days in a row.

As mentioned before, this could be a self-healing exercise or you could use it as an introduction to healing and/or include, between movements, some of the healing practices given in this book. As *Teomanía* aligns your wishes with cosmic cycles and mathematics, it could be the beginning of great change in your life.

I have been doing the 13–8 exercise for the past few years now. This is currently my fourth cycle of this exercise and the results have been amazing. I have healed many physical issues, like eye floaters, as well as deeper emotional issues and old patterns. This has become one of the foundational exercises for transformation that I use. Now I practise it not only for manifesting material things or healing, but for complete spiritual transformation. The energies are real – you can feel them. This exercise alone I have found to be life-changing.

STEVE GAUTREAU, CANADA

CHAPTER 5

The Blood Serpent

It is said that the snake is the moon's favourite pet. The moon rules over the tides and waters of our planet. Our blood is mainly composed of water, and also iron, like the Earth. According to the ancient Mexican tradition, it is a mixture of the moon and the Earth inside us, a mixture of the ruler of dreams and the ruler of the manifest world.

Of utmost importance is its colour. It is believed that when we are in our mother's womb we are dreaming of who we are and who we will become, and the light that is filtering down to us through our mother's skin while we are doing that has a reddish tone similar to the one we perceive today in X-rays and ultrasound. As we grow up, we forget this, but our unconscious does not, and it still connects a red tone to the dreams we had while we were in our mother's womb.

Moreover, in past times we were born through our mother's birth canal and emerged covered in blood. This was our first awakening in this life: we came from a world where our *nahual* governed our dreams to a world where our *tonal* governed our waking state.

Consequently, our unconscious, our cave, considers blood to be the main contact between these two states of consciousness, so when we activate the power of our blood, we are making a very powerful link between our dreams and our reality.

The following technique is known as the blood serpent, *yezcoatl* in Náhuatl, and its main function is to heal emotions.

According to the ancient Mexicans, the following emotions accumulated in the following organs:

~ *Liver:* Anger

~ *Kidneys:* Fear and guilt

~ *Stomach:* Traumas that we have not been able to digest

~ *Lungs:* Sadness and gloom

This is similar to the ideas of traditional Chinese medicine.

In the following exercise you will carry the sacred power of your blood to all these important organs. This is one of the most effective ways I know of healing emotions.

EXERCISE: THE BLOOD SERPENT

You can perform this technique as a separate practice or as part of the *Teomanía* (remember that the third movement is related to blood). You can do it standing, sitting or lying down. If you are sitting or standing, face west.

You can do this on your own, giving all the directions in the first person, or for someone else, giving the directions in the third person.

- Inhale through your nose on a count of seven and immediately exhale through your mouth on a count of seven. This completes a cycle.

- Do seven cycles. Now you have completed the first movement.

- State your intentions with the words:

  > *Ce ollin*, first movement. Through my breath, I am able to access the sacred power of my blood, the contact between *tonal* [tone-al] and *nahual* [na-wal], and activate its healing power, which will become the medicine inside me. From now on, my blood will be my medicine.

- Next, carry out another seven cycles — the second movement.

- Give the instructions for the second movement:

  > *Ome ollin*, second movement. I go deeper and deeper inside myself and activate the medicine inside myself more powerfully.

- Carry out the third set of breathing cycles — the third movement.

- Give the instructions for the third movement:

  > *Yei ollin*, third movement. I go deeper and deeper inside myself. I enter my cave and access the healing skills of my ancestors through the power of my blood.

∽ Carry out the fourth and last set of breathing cycles – the fourth movement.

∽ Give the instructions for the fourth movement:

> *Nahui ollin*, fourth movement. I have reached the sacred number of 28, the number of the moon, and with it I will activate the power of the unconscious of my own blood, bringing together the power of the waking and sleeping worlds, the conscious and the unconscious, to perform this healing.

∽ At this point, ask the power of the moon and the power of the Earth to come into your body by saying simply:

> *Metztli* [mets-li; Moon], and *Tonantzin* [ton-ant-sin; Earth], *xihualhui, xihualhui* [chi-wal-wee; come, come].

∽ Visualize the moon coming down through your crown, the Earth coming up through your feet and their energies joining in your heart.

∽ Visualize that from this joined energy there emerges a *yezcoatl*, a blood serpent. The snake is a symbol of healing in most ancient cultures. You are going to visualize the *yezcoatl* streaming through your body, healing, repairing and rejuvenating as it goes.

∽ First of all, take it to your liver. Command it to digest all the anger and damage that have accumulated there during the course of your life. Visualize it writhing for several minutes in your liver, cleaning and purifying it.

~ Then take it forward, carrying its sacred power to your kidneys. Tell it to digest all the fear and guilt you have felt in your life and heal all the damage in this area. Ask it to slither around your kidneys for a few minutes too.

~ Move on, taking the power of the blood serpent to your stomach. Have it digest all the traumas that you haven't been able to overcome in your life, as well as any kind of physical damage to your stomach. Visualize the blood serpent writhing in your stomach for a few minutes, healing and repairing your physical stomach and all your emotions.

~ Finally, carry the sacred power of the blood serpent to your lungs. Here you can visualize a single snake slithering through both lungs or have the snake divide in two and one snake go to each lung. Have it/them digest and heal the gloom and sadness in your lungs for a few minutes.

~ If you suffer from any disease in particular, for example, arthritis in the knee, you can take the blood serpent to this area and tell it to digest and heal the emotions that produced the problem. You may want to heal any damaged area in your body in exactly the same way.

~ At the end, put your hands together in front of your chest and say:

> *Ometeotl.* May my liver release all anger and heal. May my kidneys release all fear and guilt and heal. May my lungs overcome all sadness and gloom and heal. May my stomach overcome all traumas and heal. [And so on with the rest of all the organs that you have healed.] *Ometeotl.*

- Finally, tell yourself or your patient to open your/their eyes on the count of four. (If, however, you are carrying out this exercise as part of the first *Teomanía*, you should omit this step and carry on with the breathing cycles based on 13 and 8 that will take you to the next movement.)

Since beginning this work I can say that I have healed myself in so many ways, but the first step for me was to heal my emotions. I was carrying a lot of heavy energy which I had accumulated from years of drug addiction and unemployment, and the social conditioning that came with it. I felt uncomfortable in my own skin. Being honest with myself, I saw that somehow I was addicted to my own suffering and caught in the web of my old story.

After starting this work, I felt that the weight of my destructive emotions, especially my fears, lifted off me and dissolved. My relationship with myself, and with others, especially my family, improved dramatically. I also found the confidence to go to the gym again – something I hadn't done in years. This made me so happy, and also gave me more energy.

As I delved deeper into the work, I saw that a miraculous transformation was taking place, and that I was a true warrior. Love for myself and my passions in life were fully restored. I started to paint again with an energy I had never known. A few months later I was in Berlin taking part in a group exhibition. I am now a self-employed artist and daily practitioner of the art of nahualism, on the path to becoming a professional therapist and healer.

Iwan ap Huw Morgan, Wales

CHAPTER 6

The Eight Bands of Power

The wise elders of ancient Mexico saw that the primal energy of Centeotl took 13 steps to transform into the plants, animals and other life-forms of Tlalticpac, the place where we live, our physical world. They called them the 13 heavens. We will look at some of these heavens in more detail later (*see Chapter 13*).

However, it took Centeotl only eight steps, or bands, to transform into human beings. The number eight, if you remember, relates to what is hidden, and the eight bands are like the layers of an onion, with the outer one being Centeotl and the inner one being us. That is why the 13–8 cycle of the *Teomanía* exercises (*see Chapter 4*) represents the exact relationship between the cosmos and the human.

The ancient Mexicans realized that by applying this knowledge in a practical way, they could obtain amazing results.

The eight bands of power are:

The Eighth Band: *Centeotl*

This is the primal energy from which everything emanates. As mentioned earlier, the ancient Mexicans also called it Amomati, which means 'mindless mind', and Itzcuauhtli, obsidian or Black Eagle.

As Centeotl is the energy from which everything comes and to which everything returns, for healing purposes, we have to make the problem return to Centeotl so that it can be transformed once again into primal energy and disappear from our life or our client's life.

The Seventh Band: *Ometeotl*

Here Centeotl's energy is activated with the intention of creating something that will manifest in matter.

What is doing the activating? It is said to be Ometeotl, who for many is a god, but for me is the creative force in action.

It is said that the creative force has to take action: 'He who cannot create must perish.'

The Sixth Band: The Geometry of Light

When primal energy is activated, its first manifestation is in the form of light. For the ancient Mexicans, there were four basic geometric shapes of light:

- the *triangle*, representing dreams and the element of fire

68

- the *circle*, representing the old winds of our ancestors that are perpetuated through our creations and of course the physical wind, the element of air

- the *half-moon*, representing the emotions we are creating and the element of water

- the *square*, representing the Earth, and the element earth, which gives life to the entire system

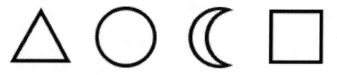

The four geometric shapes of light

This geometric order will manifest first in our dreams (triangle). If we do not dream lucidly (and most people do not), we will dream in a way that repeats the patterns of our ancestors (circle), creating the emotions (half-moon) that will turn them into matter (square).

The Fifth Band: The Luminous Sphere

All these geometric shapes will then be manifested through our luminous sphere, or aura, which is formed by the four energy bodies described in Chapter 1: *ihiyotl*, *teyolia*, *tonal* and *nahual*.

The Fourth Band: The Mould

So a mould will be created for what will become physical matter. It is this that will define its shape.

People who have developed extrasensory perception can see the mould. If you can see it, you will notice it has blue or violet tones in the areas where it is balanced and yellow, orange and red tones in the areas where it is unbalanced. Some people compare this mould to what we know nowadays as the etheric body.

The Third Band: Physical Matter

The thirds band consists of physical matter exactly as we perceive it.

The Second Band: The Four Elements

The second band consists of the energy of the four elements that make up the physical matter: air, water, fire and earth. Of course, if they are unbalanced, they will create trouble. For example, if fire isn't balanced, it will create swellings and, to a greater degree, tumours. If water isn't balanced, it will generate emotional problems or even blood conditions. If it is air that is out of balance, it will create breathing problems and repetitive life patterns. If it is earth, it will create organ degeneration, ageing and poor health, as well as difficulty in earning a living.

The First Band: Tonantzin, Mother Earth

The first band consists of the energy of Mother Earth, which holds the whole system together.

Healing with the Eight Bands

We can use the concept of the eight bands for healing. Using the technique given below, my clients have been able to heal diseases that have often been considered incurable. Many have been able to erase scars that they have carried all their life; others have lost weight in an amazing way without changing their diet. One of the most stunning cases was that of a person who later worked with me in Mexico for several years. She hurt her hand in an accident and the doctors declared she would never move it again, as the bones were too damaged. However, she practised the following technique and was able to regenerate some of the bones within a month.

EXERCISE: THE EIGHT BANDS OF POWER

PREPARATION

~ Sit comfortably with your eyes closed. (If you are performing this on someone else, ask them to do the same.)

~ Start with the breathing cycles, *Teomanía,* to induce an altered state of consciousness. (If you are healing someone else, you should perform them together.) Inhale through your nose, counting from one to 13 and drawing in all the healing power of the sun, and exhale through your mouth, counting from one to eight and expelling all the energy that is creating the problem. This is one cycle. Thirteen cycles form a movement.

~ When you finish the first movement, state your intention, for example healing hypertension or depression. You may either state this silently to yourself or out loud, but if you are healing someone else, it is better to state it out loud.

∾ Complete a second 13–8 movement.

∾ If you are healing yourself, when you have finished, start the therapeutic process (*with Step 1, below*); if you are healing another person, ask them to relax and just let the things that you will say happen to their energy.

STEP 1

∾ Visualize the problem in the area of your forehead, your *chalchiuhuitl,* jade chakra, where the union takes place between *tonal* and *nahual,* the waking and dreaming bodies. If the problem is visible, it will be easy to visualize it; if it is not visible, whatever you visualize will be correct, even if it is an abstraction such as a black cloud or a monster.

∾ Start working with the first band, which is Tonantzin, Mother Earth. Still visualizing the problem, inhale through your nose while moving your head sideways to the left.

⌁ Then exhale through your mouth while moving your head sideways to the right.

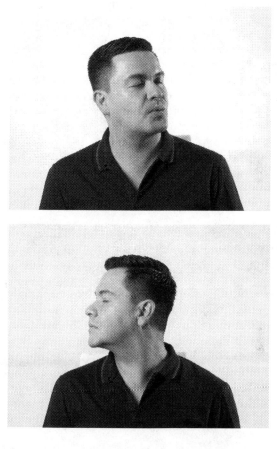

⌁ Do this process four times, asking (either verbally or mentally) Mother Earth to withdraw the energy that was sustaining the problem or disease from you or your patient.

⌁ Wait until you feel that has been done.

STEP 2

~ Then work with the second band, the four elements. Repeat the same breathing cycle: inhale through your nose and move your head sideways to the left and exhale through your mouth and move your head sideways to the right four times.

~ Ask the four unbalanced elements that are causing the problem to leave your body or your patient's body and to go back harmoniously to Mother Earth.

~ Wait a while until you feel the process has been completed.

STEP 3

~ Proceed to do the same with the third band, physical matter. However, when you carry out the breathing cycle from left to right (again four times), visualize your image of the problem turning to dust or energy. Order the problem to disappear from your life.

STEP 4

~ Repeat the four-breath cycle, visualizing the yellow, red or orange unbalanced energy that was surrounding the area you are healing being cleansed through your breaths.

STEP 5

~ Repeat the four-breath cycle, giving the command that all the discordant energy contained in the energetic fields of the *ihiyotl* [ee-yot-l], *teyolia* [tay-ol-ya], *tonal* [tone-al] and *nahual* [na-wal] are cleared so that the problem disappears.

STEP 6

⁓ Visualize in your *chachihuitl* the four geometric shapes that are creating the problem: triangle, circle, half-moon and square.

⁓ Again, do the four-breath cycle, this time visualizing that these four geometric shapes are disappearing from your forehead.

⁓ Then order the dream, the ancestral heritage and the emotions that created the problem to be removed from you (or your client).

⁓ Wait for a little while until you feel you have completely fulfilled your objective.

STEP 7

⁓ Next, visualize a symbol for *Ometeotl*, the creative energy that was the origin of the problem. The image I usually use is the double-headed serpent.

The double-headed serpent

~ Repeat the four-breath cycle while you visualize this serpent disappearing and command the creative energy that generated the problem to go away.

~ Wait for a little while until you feel the problem has dissipated.

STEP 8

~ Finally, in your mind go back to Centeotl, primal energy, put your hands together and say:

> *Ometeotl!* May the problem disappear, go back to primal energy, the mindless state, as if had never existed.

~ If you are healing another person, the moment you finish the process, give them the command to open their eyes on the count of four, now that the problem has returned to primal energy.

You can repeat this process as many times as necessary. Some people have repeated it once or twice a day for a month or more until they have reached their goals. If you are healing someone else, you could insert it into any of the movements of the *Teomanía* (*see page 49*). You could, for example, insert it into the second or fourth movement and include other techniques as well to carry out a full healing process.

I must emphasize that if you are treating several ailments at the same time, you must work on each one separately. Emotional problems can be treated the same way.

In the following testimonial, the techniques that were used were: *Teomanía* (*see page 49*), the Eight Bands of Power (*above*), Coatlicue (*see page 83*) and psychic surgery (*see page 95*):

A few months before I met Sergio at his first Ashland, Oregon, workshop, my husband, Pat, was recovering nicely from open-heart quadruple bypass surgery. However, while in the hospital, he contracted a bacterial infection that would not respond to antibiotics. The doctors recommended a second surgery to relieve the symptoms.

By the time of Sergio's workshop, Pat's skin was turning grayish and he had no energy. But it took just one session with Sergio to clear the infection. During the session Pat reports not remembering details, but, as his energy shifted, his body vibrated, and he surrendered to the process fully.

It was a joy to see the look on the doctor's face when Pat went for a follow-up exam. He had fully recovered without medicines and without surgery.

Pat is soon to be 79. His heart is healthy and his body is strong. He plays tennis four times a week.

LORI HENRIKSEN, OREGON, USA

Chapter 7

Coatlicue: Spiritual Life and Death

A nother of the techniques that has contributed to the many transformations I have witnessed in my patients as well as my students and that has gone far beyond what we consider possible is the so-called spiritual life and death.

The Sacred Black Light

The first contact I had with this wisdom so far beyond current spirituality took place many years ago after I had a lucid dream. In my dream, Popocatépetl, the most sacred mountain in Mexico, ordered me to go to the Andes so that I could learn to work with the Mexican mountains. After dreaming the same dream several times, I decided to go there, and, as I narrated in my previous book, *The Toltec Secret*, I found a tradition of the most extraordinary beauty, which genuinely honoured the mountains. Amongst the most valuable teachings that I found in Peru was something that in Quechua was called Wilkan'usta, the sacred black light. It was believed that those who were able to handle it had control over life and death.

Without any other information on it, when I came back to Mexico I had a patient called Leonardo who had a tumour in the *sella turcica*, the depression in the skull that houses the pituitary gland. This caused him first to lose his sight and later his balance. His doctors recommended he wrote his will. His cousin Ricardo, who was a friend of mine, asked me to treat him. So I started experimenting with using the sacred black light to exorcize the force of death in his tumour and taught him how to evoke it. Somewhat sceptically, he started to do it, and within two months he had recovered his balance and a few months later his vision. The doctors couldn't explain why it had happened, but the tumour had shrunk, releasing the pressure on the optical nerve, and that was why he had recovered his faculties, and moreover his life, since he could now go back to work.

I looked into whether there was something similar to the sacred black light in the ancient Mexican tradition and discovered it was the Black Tezcatlipoca. He is the force who rules the cave, the unconscious and the world of dreams and the dead, and is considered to be able to take everything from you and give you everything too. Furthermore, I found out that the force corresponding to Wilkan'usta in that it gave life and death was Coatlicue, the goddess with the skirt of snakes.

If this image is seen from the distance, it seems as if the goddess has a single head, but actually her head is formed by two snakes facing each other, symbolizing that life and death always exist together. Life starts where death ends and death starts where life ends. It is an eternal cycle of creation and destruction. As a matter of fact, in modern Mexico, twins are still called *coates* after Coatlicue, since they seem to be one but in reality they are two.

Coatlicue

Life and Death

In the cosmology of the ancient Mexicans, physical matter would always be connected to spirit or energy, since they knew there were two possible kinds of death – physical and spiritual:

~ Physical death

> In this case, matter dies; consequently, the spirit or the energy that sustained it is expelled too. This is our usual

idea of death. It is also what we are seeking when giving chemotherapy: killing each and every cancer cell.

~ Spiritual death

This consists of expelling the spirit or energy of something in the form of matter such as a tumour or a virus. The matter that formed it is expelled as well.

At the same time, our ancestors knew there were also two different ways to create life – physically and spiritually:

~ Physical life

Life is most commonly created when a sperm fertilizes an egg and this physical union attracts a spirit or energy to it.

~ Spiritual life

The opposite takes place when the energy of a certain vibration is evoked and this gives life to matter.

These are the grounds on which the technique of spiritual life and death is based. This is a technique I found that is based on the attributes of Coatlicue. I have been teaching it on my courses over the last few years. It aims to do away with the spirit or energy giving life to a problem or disease and, conversely, to create the energy that will spark life into healing or recovery on the physical plane.

EXERCISE: *COATLICUE* – SPIRITUAL LIFE AND DEATH

This technique is based on one of the greatest legacies of the Mexihca culture: the goddess Coatlicue. In the human body, her left side represents life whereas the right side represents death.

Before describing the procedure in detail, I would like to outline the technique:

~ First, we take in our left hand, the hand of life, all the energy or spirit that has been sustaining an ailment or a disease.

~ Then we put our hands together like Coatlicue, because this represents the serpent of life and death.

~ Then, using our arms as a bridge, we make this energy or spirit cross to the other side, our right side, the Mictlan, the world of the dead. Here we will ask our ancestors or the ancestors of our client to come and take that energy. We will ask them for the dream that will heal the disease.

~ Finally, we make this dream cross back into the world of the living to perform the healing.

I will describe the process as if you are healing another person, but you may perform it on yourself in just the same way.

PREPARATION

~ First of all, position your patient so that the area you are healing is in front of you.

~ Make sure you orient yourself to the geographical north of your patient, since the ancient people of Mexico believed the past and the underworlds that created problems resided in the north and therefore you have to expel the disease from this direction. (If you are healing yourself, simply orient yourself towards the north so that you can uproot any negative energy from this direction.)

~ Instruct your patient to inhale through their nose with you as you count from one to nine. Remember that nine is the number associated with the unconscious, the cave and the underworlds that create problems.

~ Then both of you exhale through the mouth, counting once again from one to nine.

~ That is one cycle; nine cycles make up one movement. I suggest you perform at least two movements before starting the healing.

~ At the end of the first movement, say something like:

> *Ce ollin*, first movement. Through the rhythm of your breathing, we are entering the inner part of you, your cave, your unconscious, to carry out healing from the very roots of your being.

~ At the end of the second movement, say something like:

> *Ome ollin*, second movement. Now we are going deeper to heal your lineage from your ancestors up to your present life. We are performing this healing in the north, so it will happen more easily.

~ Continue with the third and fourth movements if you wish.

~ One of the primary objectives of breathing in this way is for both patient and therapist to enter an altered state of consciousness. This is to eliminate any mental paradigms about what is possible and therefore allow you to perform healing, which takes place in dreams, where everything is possible.

STEP 1

~ Place yourself in front of your patient. Extending your left hand over the affected area, start to draw the energy, the spirit, of the problem and the ancestral legacy that caused the problem to your hand by saying, '*Xihualhui*.'

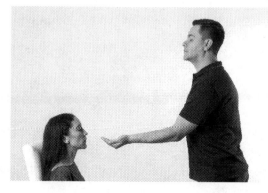

~ Keep calling the energy that has kept the problem alive. You need to feel that energy reaching your left hand. Follow your intuition as to how long you should keep pulling this energy out. Some healers have taken half an hour to gather up all the energy.

STEP 2

~ Once you feel all the energy is in your left hand, uproot it from the patient's body and then raise your hand.

~ Now, with the firm intention of killing the spirit of the problem, call Coatlicue, in the form of the serpent that kills problems, by saying, 'Xihualhui,' four times. You will immediately feel some energy reaching your left arm.

STEP 3

~ Put your hands together in front of you exactly as in the illustration of Coatlicue (*see page 81*). One represents life, the other death.

~ Now gently and easily make all the energy you were holding in your left hand cross to the right, with the firm and clear intention of bringing death to the spirit of the problem.

⌁ Once all the energy is in your right hand, separate your hands and raise your right arm.

⌁ Summon your patient's ancestors by saying 'Xihualhui' four times. They will take the energy of the disease to the Mictlan, the land of the dead, where it will no longer be able to harm the patient. Once the energy, the spirit, has been expelled, the mindset that created it will also leave, and the physical disease will follow.

STEP 4

⌁ Now summon the healing dream to your right hand by saying 'Xihualhui' four times and adding:

> I ask the dream of healing [the area affected] to come to me.

~ You will feel a special energy reaching you. Once it arrives, call Coatlicue, in the form of the energy that gives life, to give life to the dream of healing by once again saying '*Xihualhui*' four times.

~ Hold your hands together exactly as you did in Step 3 and reverse the whole process. Now you are making the healing dream that you are holding in your right hand cross from the world of dreams and the dead to your left hand, to the world of the living. Allow this to happen gently and easily.

STEP 5

~ Once you feel all the energy has crossed to the left side, raise your left arm as you did before and welcome the dream into the world of the living with some words or thoughts.

~ Very subtly, ask your patient to accept the healing.

STEP 6

~ Now put your left hand on the affected area to transmit the healing. At the same time, hold the firm intention that you are giving spiritual life to the healing and order it to live.

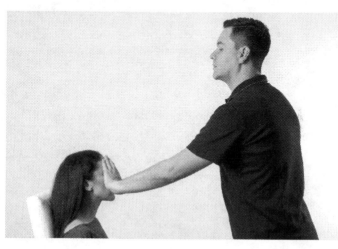

~ Once you feel that you have transmitted all the healing energy to the patient, take your hand away.

~ Next, put your hands together and say:

> *Ometeotl*, I bring spiritual death to [the problem] and I bring spiritual life to its healing. *Ometeotl.*

STEP 7

~ If this is the only healing practice you are carrying out, ask your patient to open their eyes on the count of four in a perfect state of health. If you are performing it as part of one of the *Teomanía* movements, continue with your breathing cycles and move on to the next practice.

You may carry out this process as many times as required, but not more than once a week.

To me, this technique possesses an extraordinary beauty. To give life to a dream – this is what our ancestors called a miracle.

A few years ago, I started attending Sergio's workshops in Mexico City. Undoubtedly, all of them were very insightful and useful. However, it was when I took the Andean path that I understood the importance of having that special bond with the forces of nature and the universe because of that important principle of reciprocity, especially for healing.

A few days later, my brother, a middle-aged surgeon who worked for one of the most renowned hospitals in Mexico, was infected with hepatitis C while doing surgery. Soon afterwards, severe liver damage set in and his health deteriorated. The doctors tried every single treatment, every single drug, but nothing worked and he was declared terminally ill.

In despair, I asked him if I could use one of Sergio's techniques, the Coatlicue, on him. You can imagine the look on this medical doctor's face! However, since he had nothing to lose, he agreed.

It was nerve-racking because there was no room for error. Somehow I found the courage to make a start. It took me

almost two hours to complete the process and by then my brother was asleep. I took that as a good sign.

Next day, when I went to check on him, he told me that he had had a terrible night with a piercing pain in his liver as if he had undergone real surgery. He had thought I'd made things worse, but then the pain had started to subside and he'd finally got to sleep.

I was determined to heal him, so I told him I had to repeat the process as many times as necessary. To his surprise, once I'd done it three times he started feeling better. He went back to the hospital to have his colleagues run some blood and liver tests. When they saw the results, they called him back to repeat the tests, as they thought there'd been a mistake. The second time around, the doctors still couldn't believe the results: his triglycerides levels had fallen from almost 500mg to 150mg within two weeks, the size of his liver had gone back to normal and its surface was pretty smooth.

Two months later he had fully recovered. He went back to work at the hospital that had given up on him and sent him home to die.

I believe this technique allowed me to bring death to the spirit of the disease and life to my brother's liver.

TERESA DEL VALLE, MEXICO

CHAPTER 8

Psychic Surgery

Another technique that has proved to be very successful is psychic surgery – that is, surgery on the astral plane. This is often practised by medicine men in Mexico and is very similar to some African religions where energy is transferred from an individual or an organ to an object. Some people consider it akin to faith healing.

Since I started working with this technique, I have obtained striking results with diabetes, broken bones and vision impairment, among other ailments. These results, as well as those my students have obtained, have surpassed my expectations and shattered my paradigms about what is possible. I have to conclude that this isn't a matter of faith, but a refined technique that can bring about amazing results, even in people who don't believe in it – including the therapist.

To perform psychic surgery we need the following equipment:

∽ An obsidian wand

> Obsidian is one of the most sacred stones of ancient Mexico because it is the stone of the Black Tezcatlipoca, the lord of the north, the land of the dead and land of dreams. Because obsidian comes from lava from the inside of the Earth, it is perfect for working with the underworlds that are hidden inside us. No heavy energy can escape from obsidian, so it is the best stone for healing. We use it in the shape of a wand or knife because we give it the power to kill our problems.

∽ A mixture that dries quickly

> In ancient times, clay was used in the form of a rectangle, which relates to the concept that we are made of the earth element. However, nowadays I use play-dough. This is easier to handle and has the same results.

∽ Four small obsidian, jade or white quartz stones

> You know now that to complete a 'movement' we need to perform something four times. So we also need four small obsidian stones or four small jade or white quartz stones, depending on the type of surgery that we are going to perform.

> Obsidian contains sacred black light, which is the magnetic force, as the ancients called it, capable of absorbing all the negative energy from our cave. Therefore we will be using the obsidian stones for all those ailments where there is an over-energizing force resulting in swellings, tumours (benign or malignant), pain, bodily malformations, etc.

We will be using the jade or white quartz when the ailment is a result of a lack of energy and where it is necessary to regenerate the area, as for example in all kinds of organ failure, hypothyroidism, bone and ligament regeneration, and so forth.

Obsidian wand (left), play-dough (right)
and small obsidian stones (centre)

EXERCISE: PERFORMING PSYCHIC SURGERY

I will describe the process as if you are healing another person, but you may perform it on yourself in just the same way.

PREPARATION
- Ask the patient to sit down and position them so that you are to their geographical north and the area you are going to operate on is in front of you.

⌁ Instruct your patient to inhale through their nose with you as you count from one to nine. Remember that nine is the number associated with the unconscious, the cave and the underworlds that created the problem. Then both of you exhale through the mouth, counting once again from one to nine. That is one cycle; nine cycles make up one movement.

⌁ Perform at least two movements before starting the healing.

⌁ After the first movement you can make suggestions to the patient, for example:

> *Ce ollin*, first movement. Through the rhythm of our breathing, we are entering the inner part of you, your cave, your unconscious, to carry out healing from the very roots of your being.

⌁ After the second movement, you can make a similar suggestion, and so on. You can perform up to four movements.

⌁ Take the obsidian wand in your left hand and make an opening in the patient's energetic field approximately one to two centimetres (half an inch) above the area you are going to operate on. For example, if you are going to perform eye surgery, make the opening in that area. The opening will be very close to the body, but you don't need to touch it. If something has already spread all over the body and does not have a particular location, make the opening in the solar plexus or sternum. Make sure you make the opening with your left hand and then hold it open with two fingers of your right hand.

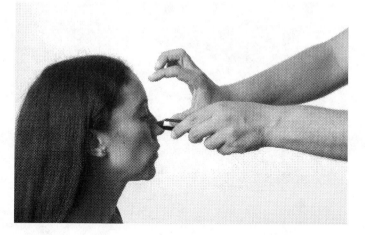

~ Now take the play-dough rectangle in your left hand. It is very important you do this with your left hand, because if you do it with your right hand, the process will fail. Remember that the left hand always receives energy, whereas the right hand projects it.

~ As you hold the play-dough in your left hand, use the tips of your fingers to feel the temperature of the energy projecting from the opening. If you feel it is hot, you will have to cool it down during the process. If you feel it is cold, you will have to heat it up before you end the process.

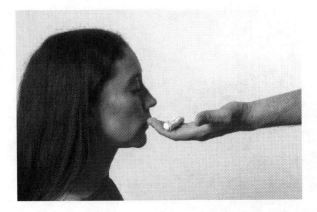

~ Start summoning the spirit, the energy that has been sustaining the disease, to the play-dough. I usually ask it to come by saying 'Xihualhui' but you may do it in your native language if you wish. Ancient languages do, however, have special power.

~ Continue summoning the energy of the disease by saying to the patient in a commanding tone of voice:

> Give me the disease. It's of no use to you anymore. You have already learned the lesson it wanted you to know.

~ As the negative energy starts to enter the play-dough, say to the patient:

> Give me the destructive patterns that created the disease. Give me the obstacles that have not been solved. Give me the emotions that created it — the anger, depression, sadness — and all the beliefs that generated it.

~ Make sure that the patient is relaxed, so they are able to release all the negative energy.

~ Keep pulling out the negative energy and repeating the words until you feel with the tips of your fingers that the temperature of the energy has changed.

~ Now you have finished pulling out the energy, but there is still a *mahui* to take care of – a string of energy that links the affected area with the play-dough. So take the obsidian wand and cut this link by moving the point between the play-dough and the affected area while saying the word *kuepa* (ku-wepa) which means 'to turn something upside down', and holding the intention that all the energy of the disease abandons the patient's body and transfers into the play-dough.

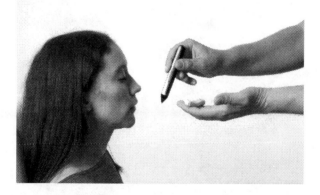

~ It is at this point that you close the energetic field. Since you have now transferred all the negative energy to the play-dough or clay, you won't continue the process in the patient's body. Visualize that you have a needle and thread in your right hand and start sewing up the opening that you made.

∽ Take the play-dough in your left hand and make sure it is long enough for you to make four incisions in it with the obsidian wand.

∽ Take the wand in your right hand, saying, '*Tecpatl* [tec-pat-l], *xihualhui.*' You are asking the power of the *pedernal,* or flint, the knife of justice, to come to your right hand.

∽ With the firm conviction that you are terminating the problem, make four incisions on the play-dough, saying, '*Miquilztli* [mi-kilts-li],' which means 'dying', followed by whatever the problem is, for example, 'Cataracts dying' or 'Kidney failure dying.' In the end, you will have four holes.

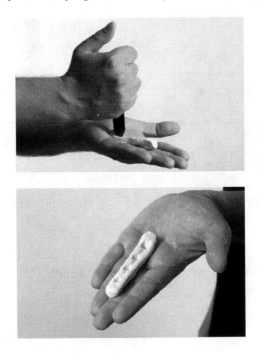

~ Move now to the south, which in the Toltec tradition represents the future and is where the willpower of the warrior is found. It is ruled by Huitzilopochtli, which means 'hummingbird flying left'. One of his many other names is Tetzahuitl, lord of the omens. Using either name, ask him to send healing by holding the four stones in your left hand while saying, '*Xihualhui, xihualhui.*' Feel the energy arriving.

~ Take the play-dough in your left hand and put the first stone into the first hole, saying to the patient, 'The first movement of your healing.'

~ Then put the second stone into the second hole, saying, 'The second movement of your healing.'

~ Continue until all the stones are in place.

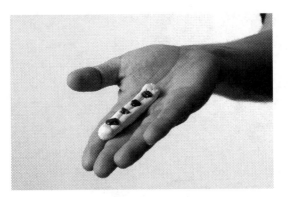

~ Now move to the east, the direction of light, the place where the most beneficial things come from. Hold your work in your hands and say:

Ometeotl, may [the problem] be solved and healing take place.

At the very end, you may hand your work to the patient or you may bury it in Mother Earth and ask her to continue the healing. If you bury it on a mountain or in a sacred place, the healing will be more powerful, but simply burying it in a flower pot may be enough.

I have had the most striking results with this form of surgery, and you may too, but if the patient has not improved within a month, you may repeat the process as many times as necessary.

In 2001, I suffered multiple head, neurological and neck injuries when roofers threw a shingle off my roof during a roof replacement in Florida. Several lingering injuries included occipital nerve damage, a shooting pain down my right arm to a point in the center of my palm, and the lack of feeling on the right side of my face. The diagnosis was permanent damage.

Fast-forward to spring 2014, when I was a volunteer in my first healing class with Sergio. As I sat on a stool with my back to the class, I remember Sergio saying to let go. I finally did let go and felt cool air leave the lower part of my skull. While he was continuing with the healing, tingly little electrical shocks started traveling from the fingertips of my right hand up the right side of my face. It was as if that side of my body was reawakening. Tears of joy were running down my face, which was not normal for me. I had feeling in the right side of my face and no shooting pains.

Several months later, I went to the doctor and was told I no longer had the permanent damage and my nerve was functioning normally. I no longer take pain medication and I have full use and feeling in my face, arm, and hand.

Sarah Mohr, USA

When my brother and I left Sergio's 'Psychic Surgery' course, he said, 'It's always good to know about these topics, but honestly I don't think we can apply them to anything useful.' We kissed goodbye and he left. He had a football match the next day.

The next afternoon he called me to say that he had torn the anterior cruciate ligament in his left knee. He couldn't even stand, much less drive. I rushed over to take him to hospital, but all of a sudden he said, 'Why don't we go to your place and you do surgery on me the way Sergio taught us yesterday?'

Of course I told him he was out of his mind and I couldn't treat something so serious with a technique that we had never used before. Nevertheless, he insisted. In the end, I thought to myself, Well, it won't matter if we get to the hospital an hour later – he'll be scheduled for surgery anyway.

I took out my notes and followed Sergio's instructions. During the process my brother told me he felt the same pain as when he had undergone 'real' surgeries. Afterwards, he fell asleep for around two hours and when he woke up he said, 'The pain has gone.' He recovered fully in two days.

You might say he hadn't torn his ligament after all, but he had torn ligaments several times before and was pretty familiar with the pain, and with post-operative pain.

Another time, I was in a remote spot on the Amalfi coast in Italy with my husband's family when Marilena, my sister-in-law's daughter, who was eight months pregnant, suffered a severe haemorrhage. We were all very scared. I approached her and asked for her permission to try an unconventional healing method until help arrived. She agreed and I started doing the first thing that came to my mind: stitching the neck of the uterus and repairing the placenta so that the baby would not be born prematurely. Shortly afterwards the haemorrhage started to diminish. Within 15 minutes it had totally stopped.

By the time the paramedics arrived, Marilena could stand up and walk. When we arrived at the hospital, the physician who examined her said it seemed as if someone had sutured her uterine neck and he could not explain how the haemorrhage had stopped.

I have performed a lot of minor psychic surgery and am currently helping a friend in Milan who has breast cancer. Distance is no hindrance.

It is true that we have great inner power and Sergio has taught me there are no boundaries.

LORELLA LEONETTI, MADRID, SPAIN

Chapter 9

Itzmitl: The Obsidian Arrowhead

I am now going to tell you about a healing technique that allows you to leave behind all the burdens of your life. It is one of the most efficient ones I know. It involves opening the doors of perception, remembering the past and healing it, and is very similar to acupuncture, but performed in a different way.

Since this is quite a demanding process, I only carry it out when I make pilgrimages in Mexico, accompanied by people from around the world, and at the end of one of the long training courses I give in Mexico. I will describe the original ritual. It can also be performed in a gentler way in a gradual step-by-step process.

The Pressure Points

First of all I will describe the pressure points on the face and neck that the ancient Mexicans worked with:

1. *The point of all the hurts of our life:* about a centimetre (half an inch) above the eyebrows, in the middle of the forehead, the point that many other traditions know as the third eye.

2. *The point of everything we have refused to see:* there are actually two of them: the hollows in each temple (you can feel them more easily when you open your mouth). In this technique, we only work with the right temple. This opens the doors to extrasensory perception.

3. *The point of everything that we have refused to hear, including the voice of our inner self:* on the lobe of our right ear.

4. *The point of the cave or the unconscious, the Black Tezcatlipoca, the inner enemy:* on the right cheekbone. As the Black Tezcatlipoca can give you everything but also take everything from you, the purpose of working with his point on the cheekbone is to transform Yaotl, the enemy, one of his many names, into Nezahualpilli, another of his names, who overcomes his weaknesses.

5. *The point of all the thoughtless words we've said:* in the centre of our chin, just below our lower lip.

6. *The point of failure and lack of power:* on the neck, at the Adam's apple.

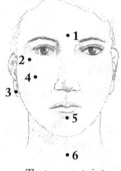

The pressure points

EXERCISE: THE OBSIDIAN ARROWHEAD AND THE MAGUEY THORN

This was originally performed in a cave, the equivalent of the unconscious. However, you can also work at home in darkness.

You will need something to apply pressure quite strongly to the points mentioned above. Obsidian has proved to be the best stone for working with the unconscious, so use an obsidian arrowhead if you can; if not, I recommend using a stone with similar properties.

If you are performing the original ritual, you will also need a thorn from the maguey plant, *Agave americana*.

An maguey thorn (left) and an obsidian arrowhead (right)

POINT 1: ALL THE HURTS OF YOUR LIFE

～ Press down strongly on this point, even if it is painful, as you recap the painful events of your life. Try to deal with the most outstanding events, such as death, tragedy, rejection, sickness, and so on.

～ Increase the pressure you are applying, because the purpose of this exercise is to replace the emotion that produced these events with one that is stronger, and that is the piercing pain of the obsidian arrowhead.

～ As you increase the pressure, there will be a moment when your body will create a natural anaesthetic effect. When this happens, give this command:

> Just as my body has stopped the pain of the obsidian arrowhead, I command all those things in my past to stop hurting me. From now on, the worst pain I have ever suffered will be the one inflicted by the obsidian arrowhead.

~ In the original ritual, we prick ourselves with the maguey thorn here, as we ask the cave for healing and offer our bravery as warriors in return.

POINT 2: ALL YOU HAVE REFUSED TO SEE

~ Press down strongly on your temple with the point of the obsidian arrowhead and think about everything you have avoided looking at in your life, everything that was there before you but you refused to see: things you were afraid to see, times when you refused to recognize that someone didn't love you or that death was approaching. Think about all these issues as you press down on this point.

~ As you press down, again there will be a moment when your body creates an anaesthetic effect. When this happens, say:

> I am not afraid of looking at anything anymore. I can face anything with the bravery of the warrior.

~ Ask the doors of your extrasensory perception to open. Know that you can look at what lies beyond without fear.

~ In the original ritual, we prick ourselves with the maguey thorn as we ask the doors of perception to open with the bravery of the warrior.

POINT 3: ALL YOU HAVE REFUSED TO HEAR

~ Apply pressure to the point on the lobe of your right ear by putting your thumb behind the lobe and the obsidian arrowhead in front of it.

~ As you press on the point, recap all the times when you have refused to listen, perhaps to the truth about a diagnosis, or someone's feelings for you, or to the still, small voice within, or the sound of silence, or the voice of your conscience.

~ Once your body has created the anaesthetic effect, say:

> May I be able to listen with bravery, the bravery of the warrior. May all the things I have refused to hear stop

hurting me. May I be able to listen to my *nahual,* my spirit and the sound of silence.

❧ In the original ritual we prick our right earlobe with the maguey thorn, ask the cave to allow us to listen to our spirit and our *nahual* and offer our bravery in return.

POINT 4: THE UNCONSCIOUS – THE INNER ENEMY

❧ As you apply pressure with the obsidian arrowhead to the point on the right cheekbone, think of all the times you've self-sabotaged, self-boycotted or let yourself down. Think about all the times when your inner self-destructive forces have been stronger than the constructive ones.

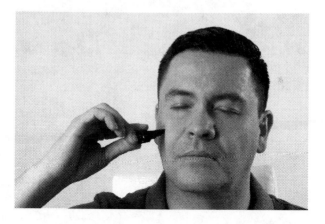

❧ Again, as you recap these issues, apply pressure until it creates the anaesthetic effect, and at that moment say:

I have defeated the inner enemy and he has now become my friend, since I have overcome darkness.

~ In the original ritual this is the moment when we prick our right cheekbone with the thorn and ask the cave to help us to defeat our inner enemy every day.

POINT 5: ALL THE THOUGHTLESS WORDS YOU'VE SAID

~ Apply pressure to the point just below your lower lip.

~ As you do so, think about all the times you've had negative thoughts about others and about yourself. Think about all the thoughtless words you've said.

~ Once you feel the anaesthetic effect, say:

> May all the negative words I've said, either about myself or others, stop having an effect. May they cease to exist.

~ In the original ritual, we prick this point with the maguey thorn and ask that all the words that we say from now on be full of wisdom.

Point 6: All your failures and lack of power

~ Press on the sixth point, located right in front of your Adam's apple, by holding the skin on one side with your thumb and pressing on the other with the obsidian arrowhead.

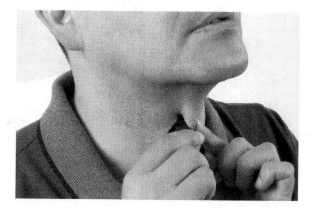

~ Press on this point, strongly, intensely, as you think of all the failures you've experienced in your life — professional, personal; perhaps addiction, loss; all the times you feel you've failed. Recap these events as you apply stronger and stronger pressure to this point.

~ Once you feel the anaesthetic effect kicking in, say:

> May all my failures stop causing me pain.

~ In the original ritual, we prick this point with the thorn to transform all the energy of our failures and all the energy of a loser into the energy of a warrior who can tackle anything, above all themselves.

If we were performing this ritual inside a cave, we would now go to the darkest part of the cave and use our peripheral vision to observe the world of energy as well as the energetic beings that our ancestors were able to see. Many of them believed that they were gods. Over five centuries later, my students and I have been able to see them again.

I gave a lot of thought to whether I should include this technique in this book. It is one of the most sacred rituals of our ancient people and belonged to the eagle and snake warriors, so I hesitated. But the time has come for all our wisdom and knowledge to return, so I have included it after all. I hope it is used wisely.

This was an amazing process. Pressing the obsidian arrowhead numbed the area before we pierced our skin with the agave thorn. I was able to release the heavy energy of things I had been told in my childhood, the hurtful words I had said to myself and others and the failures of my life. I had a blank slate and was ready to forgive myself and set out on a new path of enlightenment. I realized I was tougher and stronger than I had imagined.

Upon finishing the exercise, we went into a dark area of the cave we were working in. As I sat quietly, I began to realize I could see the raw energy of the cave. There was twinkling white light everywhere I looked. Then I saw the energy of the man of the cave [a spirit guardian].

The next energetic body I saw was that of the feathered coyote [guardian of nahualism and the caves of power] pacing back and forth in front of me. As I acknowledged his presence, he came up to me, wrapped his front paws around my neck and we hugged. That was amazing!

RICK MAURMANN, OREGON, USA

PART II

Rejuvenation

CHAPTER 10

Symbols from the Land of Dreams

A fter some years of exploring the healing and energy worlds and shattering my ideas of what was possible in the process, I felt the need to go beyond what I knew. The next goal was rejuvenation.

Why did I decide to explore this area? Most people on the spiritual path have heard stories of yogis hundreds of years old and occult masters who have stopped ageing altogether. There were stories like that in Mexican nahualism too, and I wanted to prove them true.

Symbols for Rejuvenation

I found theories about rejuvenation, but at first I couldn't find any practices, so I did some research into the subject and once again used the lucid dreaming state to ask how to do it. It was then that some symbols were shown to me:

✳ 👁 𝟢 990

I had no idea what they meant, but they were brought to me directly from the Mictlan, the land of dreams and the dead, so I offered them to my students as a rejuvenation technique, not knowing if it would really work. At that time I was really young, so I didn't experiment on myself.

Afterwards, many of my students were able to lose their aches and pains, recover from illnesses and regain their original hair colour just by drawing the symbols, with intent, on labels and putting them on shampoo, moisturizing lotion and so forth, or on glasses of drinking water, or directly on the affected areas, and I saw with my very own eyes that it was possible to reverse ageing in normal people, people I knew.

The problem was that it only happened to 20 per cent, although more or less 80 per cent experienced amazing healings.

Still, my students had demonstrated to me that rejuvenation was possible through the use of symbols. Later studies I carried out brought forth the ancient rejuvenation techniques that I will share here. These have proven to be effective with a lot of people.

Xochitl: The Flower

One of the techniques I found has now had amazing results all over the world. It is based on the ancient Mexicans' use of the flower as a metaphor for the universe.

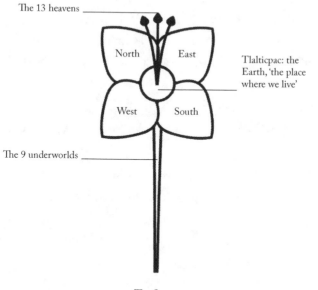

The flower

The Parts of the Flower

- *The centre of the flower* is called *Tlalticpac* and it represents the place where we live, our material reality. When it comes to healing and rejuvenating techniques, *Tlalticpac* is our physical body, the place where our spirit resides.

- *The north petal* is the *Mictlan*, the land of the dead and the ancestors. It was believed that all our ancestral influences, which we now know as genetics, lay in the north of our energetic field. We need to make modifications here in order to rejuvenate and heal.

∽ *The west petal* is called *Cihuatlampa*, the place of feminine energies. Its main characteristic is that it is the place of rejuvenation. Unfortunately, because of our beliefs and collective paradigms, we are programmed to get older by the day. We need to run a different program and become younger and healthier by the day.

∽ *The south petal, Huitzlampa*, is the place of the hummingbird, which is considered an extraordinary bird since it is able to do things that other birds cannot do, such as fly backwards and hover in the air. So in this petal we can program ourselves to do things that others might consider impossible, such as rejuvenating. We can also remove the thorns on our path, that is to say eliminate the stress and worry that make us age more quickly. We learn to solve all our difficulties here, since this is the place of the waters, which govern our emotions. Healing our anger, sadness, fear and blame is a vital part of rejuvenation.

∽ *The east petal* is *Tlauhcopa*, the place of light and precious knowledge. It is here that we align ourselves with our magnificent destiny of enlightenment.

∽ *The stamens* of the flower are the 13 heavens, which represent the 13 steps of transforming primal energy into matter (*see Chapter 13*). In the flower exercise, we have to command the 13 heavens to reconfigure the program we run so that we become healthier and can regenerate our body organ by organ and cell by cell.

∽ *The stalk and the roots* are the cave, the unconscious, the underworlds where our mind is trapped. There are many programs and patterns here that we need to change before we can rejuvenate:

- all the destructive and repetitive patterns that we are experiencing, for example a relationship that isn't working, a bad job, an addiction, etc.

- the obstacles that are preventing our body from moving to another reality

- the laziness, lack of discipline or fear of change that is preventing us from getting results and reaching our goals

- the beliefs or paradigms – medical, social or religious – that are preventing us from healing or rejuvenation

- our ancestral heritage

- our destructive emotions

- our inability to lucid dream (as our dreams may be the cause of our ageing). (However, with this exercise we may be able to change the way we dream.)

- the part deep within us that believes the rules of the material world are the only reality. We need to abandon this belief and enter a more flexible world where we can manifest what we want.

EXERCISE: THE FLOWER

In this exercise, you address all these areas: you heal your body, modify your genetics, change your beliefs, eliminate your problems, align with your destiny, gain knowledge, reconfigure your mental paradigms and heal your underworlds.

THE POSTURE

~ Put your left foot behind you and reach upwards with your arms. They represent the stamens of the flower. Your body is the centre of the flower and your energetic field the four petals.

~ Now put both feet together. Energetically, you have assumed the posture of the flower.

Recently I made a trip to Egypt, and there I saw the same posture, but in someone who was carrying the universe. I was nevertheless delighted to see the similarity with the flower posture, as the purpose of the flower is to synchronize us with the movement of the universe. The ancient Mexicans believed that the only reality that existed was *ollin*, movement, and 'Toltec' comes from the word *tolli*, which means 'measure'. So 'Toltec' means 'the ones who know the measure of the movement of the cosmos'.

SPINNING

~ Now spin to the left for 18 minutes.

The purpose of spinning is to execute a geometrical repetitive movement that synchronizes you with the measure and movement of the universe, so that later on you can command that energy to rejuvenate and heal you.

Counterclockwise is the opposite direction to the way time moves. That's why we spin to the left.

Why 18 minutes? Because in ancient Mexico, people divided time differently. Each day consisted of 20 fractions and each fraction consisted of 72 minutes. If you add this up, it turns out to be the 24 hours of our modern time. Moreover, as you now know, the entire ancient Mexican system was based on the number four. A fourth of the 72-minute fraction is 18 minutes, which is long enough to make changes.

~ At the same time as you are spinning, state, either mentally or verbally, all your intentions. Address all your own problems, addictions, emotional difficulties, and so on, saying:

My 13 heavens are rejuvenating me. I am repairing all my organs one by one [mention them one by one]. I am healing all my diseases.

I am aligning with precious knowledge.

I am rejuvenating, and I look younger every day. I am turning my grey hair back to its original colour [if necessary]. I am losing weight [if necessary].

I am healing my emotions. I am changing anger into forgiveness, sadness into happiness, fear into certainty. I am happier every day.

I command all the obstacles on my path to disappear.

I am healing my ancestors. I am healing my genetic heritage.

I am moving away from destructive patterns. I am doing away with laziness, fear and lack of discipline.

I am changing my beliefs and breaking free of any mental limitations.

I have lucid dreams and am able to rejuvenate through my dreams.

I heal and rejuvenate.

~ Give these commands clearly and firmly. There is no point in spinning if you aren't giving the commands with authority. Repeat them for 18 minutes.

~ Once you have completed the 18-minute cycle, come to a gentle halt, still in the same position.

~ Ask the *tolli*, the measure and movement of the universe, to come to you by saying, '*Xihualhi.*' Receive this energy through your arms, which are acting as the stamens of the flower.

~ Order it to heal and rejuvenate you by saying:

Ometeotl. [Mention your personal needs once again.] *Ometeotl.*

~ Repeat this process for at least 52 days.

129

Remember that according to the ancient Mexicans, 52 is the number that is connected to the perfect alignment of Orion's Belt, an event that takes place every 52 years. Hence it brings a new cycle, a new dream, the new fire — a body that rejuvenates and heals.

My husband, Noel, and I have done three cycles of spinning and continue to be amazed at the results. Besides the calmness that we have gained from this meditation, Noel is regaining his hair, my own hair has started going back to its original red, and both of us have drastically reduced our wrinkles. The places where Noel's head was completely smooth now have hair sprouting all over them. One day my young niece was over and positioned herself on the couch to look down at Noel's head. When he asked what she was doing, she responded, 'Watching your hair grow.'

At that point, neither of us had spoken to anyone about the changes we had been experiencing.

At work one of my colleagues, who hadn't seen me in a year, commented on how much he liked my new hair colour. All I had been doing was using the techniques Sergio had taught us.

The most dramatic change I have experienced came only a month ago, after my third cycle of spinning: hip pain that I had had for 10 years completely subsided.

It still amazes us how an ancient Toltec rejuvenation practice, performed for just 18 minutes a day, has allowed us to transform our bodies and our lives.

Maxine Tezcacoatl and Noel Ollinacatl, Canada

I was diagnosed with rheumatoid arthritis in 2009 and Lyme disease in 2010. After several trials on very serious drugs such as methotrexate, hydroxychloroquine and sulfasalazine, the inflammation markers in my body had not improved; in fact they had got worse. So I was put on steroids and opioid drugs. The prognosis was awful and depressing.

Around that time I met Sergio Magaña Ocelocoyotl in London and read his first book, The Dawn of the Sixth Sun. *I felt the information was logical, simple and powerful, so I started doing the exercises every day. Well, most days, as I wasn't well enough sometimes. Despite my lack of discipline, my general health improved. I was able to get off the opioid painkillers, and the steroids too, and I felt alive and most importantly hopeful again. I also found doctors with a different approach to Lyme who could help me even more.*

About half a year later, Sergio came back to London to teach rejuvenation exercises. The class was very interesting but intense, and for me, a bit tiring. So I decided to continue with just the easiest exercise, the spinning. I practised by myself at home daily.

A couple of weeks later I visited my family in Hungary and decided to talk about my experiences. My audience asked me to practise the spinning with them, so we did it together – about 20 ladies. It was an amazing feeling! I also had great feedback from the participants.

When I arrived back home, I visited my rheumatologist and had my regular blood test. A few weeks later I was recalled for another test because the first one was 'too good' to be true without drugs! The second one was even better: apart from one inflammation marker, everything was perfect, and still is now.

My most recent Lyme blood test showed only one strain of borrelia [parasite] with slight positivity as opposed to six different strains three years ago.

I am eternally grateful for the Toltec teachings!

María Lampert, UK/Hungary

CHAPTER 11

Ohmaxal: The Cosmic Cross

There is another rejuvenation technique that has had stunning results. I will share it with you now. I believe it is a great treasure. I'm so glad I met the teachers who could explain it to me.

The Cosmic Cross

The Cosmic Cross is a symbol that has appeared in many different cultures, including the ancient Egyptian, Hindu, Mayan and Templar traditions.

The ancient cultures in Mexico interpret this symbol as follows. Centeotl, the primal energy from which we all originated and to which we will all return, lives in the 13th heaven. It is also known as Amomati, mindless state, and Itzcuauhtli, Black Eagle.

Black Eagle splits into Ometecuhtli and Omecihuatl, Mr Two and Mrs Two, the Mexican equivalent of the dual forces of yin and yang. Ometecuhtli and Omecihuatl have four children, who are all named a variant of Tezcatlipoca, smoking mirror.

In the original tradition the Tezcatlipocas were named essences, energies that were inside and outside us, then, with the coming of religion, this degenerated into calling them gods. Each governs a moment of the day, a moon phase, a solstice or equinox. Thus their eternal movement is what gives form to what we know as time.

These are the Tetzcatlipocas and their attributes:

~ *Yayauhqui Tezcatlipoca*, the Black Tezcatlipoca

He was the first Tezcatlipoca to be born. He governs the north petal, the land of the dead and dreams, and the cave, the unconscious. He is also the ruler of midnight, the new moon and the autumn equinox.

~ *Tlatlauhqui Tezcatlipoca*, the Red Tezcatlipoca

He was the second Tezcatlipoca to be born. He governs the west petal of the flower, the place of renewal and feminine energy. He is also called Xipe Totec and is the one who sets the Black Tezcatlipoca's dream in motion in the universe. He is the energy of renewal and the ruler of sunset, the waning moon and the spring equinox.

~ *Texouqui Tezcatlipoca*, the Blue Tezcatlipoca

The third Tezcatlipoca governs the south petal of the flower, the place of discipline and repetitive patterns. He rules repetitive patterns in the cosmos and also repetitive patterns in people. He is also known as Huitzilopochtli. He is the ruler of dawn, the crescent moon and the winter solstice.

    Quetzalcóatl, the White Tezcatlipoca

      The fourth Tezcatlipoca governs the east petal of the flower, the place of light and precious knowledge. He rules midday, the full moon and the autumn solstice.

Most people attributed divine qualities to the Tezcatlipocas. However, people of higher knowledge knew that there was a place in the 12th heaven called Ontlaixco where these essences converged to form the sacred geometry of the ancients as well as the famous Cosmic Cross.

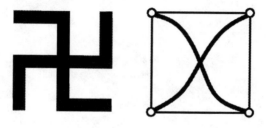

The Cosmic Cross

In this figure Ometecuhtli and Omecihautl represent the two lines of energy known as the father's and the mother's thinking. Later, their four children unite them, forming a square that when put into motion creates the cross.

Spinning clockwise (to the right), the cross moves time forward. Some of the most vivid representations that we Mexicans have of this are the so-called Voladores de Papantla, the flying men of Papantla. They are four men who hang from a rope by their feet and spin. Although academics (and others) refuse to believe it, this act is based on the Cosmic Cross principle.

Voladores de Papantla, the flying men of Papantla

For rejuvenation and healing, we can invert the process by moving the Cosmic Cross counterclockwise (to the left).

EXERCISE: TURNING THE COSMIC CROSS COUNTERCLOCKWISE

~ Sit down comfortably facing east and visualize the Cosmic Cross, whose energy is already inside you, right in the centre of your sternum, moving clockwise like a windmill.

~ Concentrate on one of the blades of the cross, the upper one, and start spinning the cross counterclockwise. Start very slowly and gradually increase the speed until the blade reaches its lowest point. Now say, 'Rejuvenation.'

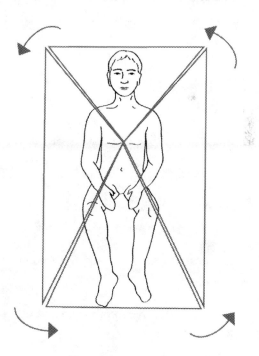

- ∾ Spin it once again and when it reaches its lowest point mentally say, 'Regeneration.'

- ∾ Spin it once again and say, 'Hair colour restoration' (if you need this). Continue in this way with whatever rejuvenation you need.

- ∾ Increase the speed of the cross until you feel the energy is moving as fast as a four-blade fan.

- ∾ Remember that each of these blades represents one of the Tezcatlipocas, who in turn represents one of the measures of time. Hence, when the Cosmic Cross is spinning very quickly, start moving time backwards in your mind with the firm intention of healing and rejuvenation. For example:

  - Night, sunset, midday, dawn, previous night, sunset, midday, dawn...

  - 2016, 2015, 2014, 2013, 2012...

  - December, November, October, September, August...

  - Sunday, Saturday, Friday, Thursday...

  - Full moon, crescent moon, new moon, waning moon, full moon, crescent moon, new moon, waning moon...

  - Winter solstice, autumn equinox, summer solstice, spring equinox...

  - Now, youth, childhood, womb, now, youth, childhood, womb...

Just as with the previous exercise, perform it for 18 minutes and, if you want the best results, at least 52 days.

When you are performing this technique, you can hold water containers in your hands. The water will be impregnated with the properties of healing and rejuvenation. Then you can drink it.

Results vary from individual to individual; however, I have had sick patients who have gone to the moment before they got ill and have experienced amazing healing. Others have preferred to use this technique to erase past traumas, diseases, accidents, abuse, etc. Some have rejuvenated, while others have changed their life in other ways. The most spectacular results have come from people who have seen great changes in 52 days and have kept on going.

In May 2013 I attended two workshops by Sergio. These courses opened up a new world to me. I noticed that the way I interacted with life started to change, as did the way life interacted with me… My physical and emotional health started to improve through the practices as well as through new health practitioners emerging to help. Difficult relationships began improving within my family and co-workers, and more abundance arrived (new jobs for my husband).

In March 2015, I attended Sergio's rejuvenation workshop. I began doing the flowering rejuvenation exercise for 52 days as required, and felt better and better. I decided then that since I was older (early fifties) and had a few physical and emotional issues needing attention, I would do four movements of it. So I did it 208 days in a row, asking for physical and emotional healing, the healing of my ancestors, and to meet the right people and have the right experiences for my flowering.

One of the first changes I noticed was that getting over jet lag was much easier. I barely had any jet lag when I traveled to Europe, sleeping well from the first night (normally a five-day process for me). I became a more easy-going person and found it much easier just to 'go with the flow'. I had the strength and discipline to stay on a rigorous healing diet (both at home and through nine weeks of travel). I laugh more often now and life is full of greater joy.

The daily practice became a supportive meditation where I could address clearing my path of thorns. I would often hold the intention of healing of my ancestors and bloodline too. I am from a large family and since there are so many of us there are quite a few mental and physical health issues. Since I have completed my practice, one family member has finally left her abusive husband and got a divorce. Another, who suffers from seasonal affective disorder, has had her healthiest winter in a long time. Another finally decided to have a hip-replacement surgery. I cannot say for sure that these events were due to clearing the ancestral line, but it does leave you wondering.

One day last November as I was doing the Cosmic Cross rejuvenation practice, I had a moment of doubt and wondered if it had really had an impact on my life. Within 20 minutes of that thought there was a knock at the front door. The mail

man was there with a registered letter saying that my husband would be receiving the money that he was owed by his previous company. Was that just coincidence? I don't think so.

ELIN GWYN, ONTARIO, CANADA

In 2015 I was diagnosed with a breast tumour. The doctor suggested surgery and radiation treatment, but I thought that there had to be another way to regain my health.

After meeting Sergio and attending one of his workshops, I worked with my dreams and underworlds and learned how to cleanse my cave.

Six months later, when I went back to my doctor for a check-up, my tumour had gone. My doctor didn't believe it was possible without treatment, but had to admit there had been a spontaneous remission.

After that, I attended Sergio's rejuvenation workshop and did a cycle of exercises for 52 days. Well, I had a wonderful result. I am 52 years old and I look 35. My friends have asked me if I have had plastic surgery.

I am still spinning and doing the cross exercise. I am healthy and I feel great.

STEFANIA, ITALY

Stefania hasn't stopped doing the exercises, and really the results are spectacular.

CHAPTER 12

The Ritual of the Full Moon

The ancient Mexicans, who were great observers of the cosmos, realized that ageing was directly related to the eternal flow of what we now call time. However, their observations went further, since they realized that in normal circumstances, a woman's lifespan was longer than that of a man, something that we are seeing again today. They concluded that this was down to one particular factor: menstruation. They claimed that women had a monthly opportunity to purify themselves of all the emotional energy that had been trapped in the organs we mentioned earlier – anger in the liver, sadness in the lungs, etc. They also observed that the moment women stopped menstruating, they began to age more rapidly. So they created a ritual, almost unknown today, for men to rid themselves of negative energy and women to avoid deteriorating after the menopause. It could also be performed as a rejuvenation practice.

EXERCISE: THE RITUAL OF THE FULL MOON

This ritual is very similar to that of *yezcoatl*, the blood serpent (*see page 60*). You should perform it at full moon.

- Close your eyes, inhale through your nose on a count of seven and exhale through your mouth on a count of seven. This completes a cycle.

- Seven cycles form a movement. Complete four movements to reach the number 28, the number of the moon.

- Visualize the moon coming down through your crown, the Earth coming up through your feet and both interweaving in your heart to create a *yezcoatl*, a blood serpent, which will travel through your body, healing and repairing as it goes, and come back to your heart.

- First of all, take it to your liver. Command it to digest all the anger and damage that have accumulated there during the course of your life. Visualize it writhing for several minutes in your liver, cleaning and purifying it.

- Then take it to your kidneys. Tell it to digest all the fear and guilt you have felt in your life and heal all the damage in this area. Visualize it slithering around your kidneys for a few minutes.

- Take it to your stomach and have it digest all the traumas that you haven't been able to overcome in your life, as well as any kind of physical damage to your stomach. Visualize it writhing in your stomach for a few minutes.

~ Then take it to your lungs. Remember that you can visualize a single snake slithering through both lungs or have the snake divide in two and one snake go to each lung. Have it/them digest and heal the gloom and sadness in your lungs for a few minutes.

~ If you suffer from any other disease or damage, take the blood serpent to this area and tell it to digest and heal the emotions that produced the problem.

~ Now visualize the serpent moving through your heart and command it to digest any ageing in the heart and any heart damage.

~ When you feel this happening, count one.

~ Visualize the serpent in your heart once again and command your heart rate to slow down and the serpent to remove all the energy that has aged.

~ Then count two.

~ Visualize the serpent in your heart again, slow down your heart rate again, deepen your breathing and count three.

~ Repeat this process, in a slow and measured way, until you have counted 13.

~ By this time you will more or less be in what the ancient Mexicans called the state of dreaming while awake. Your body will feel paralysed, as it is when you are dreaming while asleep, and your hands and feet will feel heavy, as if you can't move them. Everything you do in this state will go deep into your cave and have much more power than ordinary visualization.

~ Without opening your eyes, have the serpent in your heart move to your left index finger and break the paralysis of the dream by moving it smoothly up and down.

~ Take a needle in your right hand, or something else you can prick yourself with to draw blood. In the original ritual a maguey thorn is used.

~ Prick your left index finger to get a drop of blood. As it emerges, command:

> May my blood make all the rage, fear, trauma, sadness, sickness and ageing go away and purify and rejuvenate my whole body.

~ Once you have a big enough drop on your finger, use it to draw the symbol of the four movements on Tonantzin, Mother Earth:

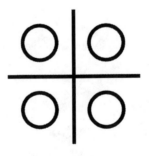

The four movements

⌒ Then tell the Earth that you're offering your blood in order
to rejuvenate and heal.

This ritual is performed once a month, on the day of the full
moon or a day before or after (as the full moon's influence lasts
throughout this period). However, you can perform it for three
days in a row if you wish. Remember that 'three' in Náhuatl is
yei, which comes from *yeztli*, 'blood'. So, to act in line with the
sacred mathematics, don't perform this kind of ritual for longer
than three days.

I would like to add that I've used this ritual for a long time to
keep my body free from sickness and the effects of time.

---

*In the course of researching many ancient forms of spirituality,
I came across the information that in several ancient cultures
certain men and women knew how to reverse the ageing process.
Their goal was to live long enough to fulfil their soul's destiny
without having to go back through the cycle of life, death and
rebirth. When I was 55, I began to say, 'When I turn 60, I'm
going to find out how the ancients did their age-reversal so I can
do it too!'*

*I turned 60 on April 21, 2014. By then, my knees were
increasingly painful and my weight was making it more and
more difficult to get around. On my last trip with Sergio to
Mexico I had been so heavy and out of shape and my knees had
been so bad that I had not been able to climb the Sun Pyramid
to do a ceremony.*

Over 2014 I just kept getting worse. By November I was wearing knee braces and taking so much pain medication I was worried about my liver. Climbing was almost impossible and of course my weight was going up. My chiropractor and physician were encouraging me to see a surgeon.

I discovered that I had insulin resistance and began to take charge of my endocrine system. My weight began to come down, but my right knee was still agonizing. I finally went to my family doctor at the beginning of 2015 and he said that there was nothing holding my knee in place. X-rays showed I had moderate to severe arthritis in both knees. The doctor arranged for an MRI scan and made an appointment with the surgeon for the first week of May. That gave me five weeks to find a miracle.

I attended Sergio's age-reversal course and afterwards was diligent with the practices. Each day I began to get better. I began to research the supplements that were required to assist my recovery and I took them. It was as if the entire universe was supporting the process.

Some of the best words I've ever heard came when I went to the surgeon and he said to me, 'Laura, I'm sorry, but I can't read your MRI.'

Horrified, I replied, 'But I didn't move an inch!'

He said, 'No, it was very clear, but I can't read it.'

Confused, I said, 'But why?'

He said, 'If you had come to me after the X-ray, we would have been looking at a very serious surgery, but this isn't the same knee. In fact I can't really see any problem with it.'

I was ecstatic. 'You mean I don't have to have surgery?'

He replied, 'No, not if you are not having any pain or other issues. Keep doing what you're doing.'

Now, just over a year later, I have completed 365 days of age-reversal. I have lost over 50 pounds and am walking, climbing and even jumping. People are shocked when I tell them that I will be 62 this year. When I went back to Mexico in the December of 2015, not only did I make it up the Sun Pyramid, but I was first to the top.

I am free now and the future is wide open.

LAURA HEMING, CANADA

PART III

Manifestation

CHAPTER 13

The 13 Heavens

After exploring the world of healing and rejuvenation for some years and having some spectacular results, I realized that, despite having made positive changes in myself, I was still lacking some things I had always wanted to manifest, such as a house and a relationship. Obviously, the next step was to explore the world of manifestation and positive thinking.

With my first teacher, Laura Muñoz, I had obtained some manifestation results with the power of candles. However, I took a significant step forward in the Andes when I learned of the ceremonies of the ancient *paqos* known as *despachos*. *Despachos* ceremonies involve making a kind of small mandala through which you send your thoughts, feelings and actions out from the Earth to all the forces of the universe, which will reciprocate by giving you something in return. That was when I understood the importance of ritual.

In Mexico, I knew about the great ceremonies where dances took place around a ritual offering for hours and hours. They were breathtaking. But they were tough to execute on your own. I also knew there was a ritual tradition in Teotihuacán, whose slogan was 'the place where men become gods' or 'the place where men become energy'. So I figured that the ancient rituals of manifestation still existed, but they were well hidden.

That turned out to be true. For the ancient Mexicans, it was dreams that created the events of the waking world, so their rituals were mostly found in *nahualismo*, the dreaming tradition, although there were also some rituals that belonged to the *tonal*, the waking world. I started experimenting with them, and from then on, everything I created either manifested or, if it didn't, something better came along instead. So if I asked for something special and it didn't manifest, I could rely on something better arriving soon.

I have chosen three rituals to give you in this section. One belongs to the dream world, another involves cosmic mathematics and the last one explores the caves of power. I recommend you carry out the *Teomanía (see pages 49–57)* or the healing exercises *(in Part I)* before you start on the manifestation exercises, however, so that your underworlds do not interfere with the manifestation process.

I hope your dreams come true!

The 13 Heavens

As mentioned previously, the ancient Mexicans believed in the existence of 13 heavens. They stated that primal energy, Centeotl, the Black Eagle or mindless state, took 13 steps to transform into what we call matter, the Tlalticpac, the place in which we live. So, the 13 heavens are dimensions, if you like, that provide us with the energy to manifest the world of matter.

Now, when we analyse these heavens, we see they were of utmost importance to the ancient Mexicans, especially the Teotihuacáns, Toltecs and Mayans. The same is true for the Andeans and their *despachos*, the offerings that go from the Earth to the stars. They saw the cosmos not as separate from the workings of reality but as an integral part of it. So when I see information that claims to be Toltec or Mayan but is related neither to cosmic mathematics nor to the dream world, I always question its origins, since it was these cosmic systems that underpinned these cultures. Moreover, this was also true for the Sumerians, Babylonians and Egyptians.

I will describe the 13 heavens in the simplest possible way so that you can understand them and then use them to create the life you want in conjunction with the forces of the universe.

Before beginning the explanation, I would like to point out that eight of the heavens are energetic. If you remember, eight is the number of things that are hidden in the dark of night, things that cannot be seen. The other five heavens are physical, and five is the number making ideas reality through our five fingers. It is the number of creation in the physical world. So the cosmology is in perfect accordance with its mathematical foundations.

These are the 13 heavens:

~ *The 13th heaven:* This is where you find primal energy, Centeotl, the energy from which everything comes and to which everything returns. The concept of separation is actually an illusion. We are all Centeotl. I am Centeotl who had the idea of transforming into me; the computer I'm writing on is Centeotl who had the idea of becoming a computer, and so on with everything that exists.

~ *The 12th heaven:* This is where Centeotl transforms into his first two creations, Ometecuhtil and Omecihuatl, Mr and Mrs Two. So it is in this heaven that the ideas that are going to exist take form, metaphorically, through the sound of the conch and the smoke of the *sahumador*, the smudging pot. You can visit this heaven to create the things you wish to manifest (*I will explain this process later on*).

~ *The 11th heaven:* This is where the children of Mr Two and Mrs Two live, the four Tezcatlipocas. When you are in this heaven, you can ask them for the things you want. Ask the black one to heal your dreams and your unconscious mind, ask the red one for physical healing, ask the blue one for will and discipline, and ask the white one for precious knowledge. This is a very important heaven, but for manifestation it is better to go to the 12th heaven.

~ *The 10th heaven – the red heaven:* This is where you repair, regenerate and rejuvenate your body, because, as we learned earlier, when you were dreaming in the womb, your body was being formed in the reddish light that was permeating through your mother's skin, and so your unconscious mind associates the colour red with the creation of the physical body.

~ *The ninth heaven – the blue heaven:* Many traditions say we come from the stars and that we all have a guiding star. In the Andes, they call it Apu Estrella Guia – Apu Guidance Star. In the Christian tradition a star guided the Magi to the baby Jesus. In our tradition, our guiding star is not a particular star, but refers to the ninth heaven, the heaven of stellar wisdom.

~ *The eighth heaven – the golden heaven:* This is the heaven of the sun's *nahual* – the spirit of the sun before the physical sun existed. According to the ancient Mexicans, it normally manifests as an eagle or jaguar. It is common in ancient cultures to have different manifestations of the sun; in Egypt, for example, they have the scarab, solar disc and falcon. The ancient people of knowledge went to this heaven in dreams or altered states of consciousness in search of their destiny.

~ *The seventh heaven – the white heaven:* This is the heaven of the moon's *nahual* – the spirit of the moon before the physical moon existed. For us, the moon is one of the representations of the Black Tezcatlipoca. It can give us both fortune and disgrace. It is best to go to this heaven alongside the 12th for physical manifestation.

~ *The sixth heaven – the heaven of movement:* The Cosmic Cross resides here, the cross that keeps everything moving.

~ *The fifth heaven:* Here we cross the frontiers of the physical universe. Comets and shooting stars are part of this heaven, reminding us that everything is moving.

~ *The fourth heaven:* This is the heaven of all the physical stars. It is said that half of them are allies of the sun and the other half are allies of the moon, so they represent the dualism of day and night, *tonal* and *nahual.*

~ *The third heaven:* Venus resides in this heaven. Venus was considered to be the star of the *tonal* at dawn as well as the star of the *nahual* at night, apparently dividing our existence into two realities, the waking world and the world of dreams.

~ *The second heaven:* The heaven of the physical sun, Tonatiuh.

~ *The first heaven:* The ancient Mexicans referred to this heaven as the 'invisible prison of the moon', because of its direct influence on us. It is the heaven of the physical moon, winds and clouds. Winds bring good and bad times, while clouds bring emotional changes and are governed by the moon, which rules the waters. That is why it is vital for our consciousness to travel beyond this heaven if we wish to live a more stable life.

EXERCISE: MANIFESTING
THROUGH THE 13 HEAVENS

I recommend doing this exercise at night, before you fall asleep, when you are entering what science now calls the hypnagogic state.

~ Lie down comfortably in your bed and do the breathing cycles I taught you in Chapter 5 (*see page 60*), four cycles of seven to make 28, the number of the moon, the guardian of dreams.

﹋ Create the blood serpent inside yourself as before, but this time, instead of taking it to all your organs, let it go straight to your heart and begin to slow your heartbeat while counting one, two, and so on, as I explained in the Ritual of the Full Moon (*see page 144*).

﹋ When you have counted to 13 and feel your hands are half-paralysed, take the serpent in your heart to your forehead and make it come out through your jade chakra, *chalchiuhuitl*, where your *tonal* and *nahual* unite. This is commonly shown in depictions of ancient Egyptian pharaohs; I suppose they had a similar discipline.

﹋ Now make that snake go out of the room, up into the air, through the clouds and the winds, and on past the moon. Tell it that you will no longer live in duality. Crossing the clouds heals your emotions and going beyond the moon overcomes your invisible prison of lunar duality.

﹋ In your dreaming state, go beyond the sun, Venus, the stars, the comets and into the sixth heaven, where you will find the Cosmic Cross.

﹋ Keep going up and enter the seventh heaven, the moon's heaven. Ask to see the *nahual* of the moon.

﹋ However the *nahual* appears to you is okay. It could appear as an animal or a woman with eyes without the iris. In fact this is the way to recognize her. Offer her your friendship and ask in return for all you want to manifest. Try to get along with the moon in a delightful way.

~ Now leave the moon's heaven and move upwards through the heaven of the sun's *nahual* and the heaven of the stars and into the 10th heaven, the red heaven. If you need healing, stay there for a while regenerating your body.

~ Then go up through the heaven of the Tezcatlipocas and into the 12th heaven, where Ometecuhtli and Omecihuatl live. Ask to see them.

~ However the couple of creation appear to you is fine. Sometimes I've seen them as one of my teachers and his wife, sometimes my parents. I've even seen them as two trees.

~ Once you have met Mr and Mrs Two, ask them to create something for you with the sound of the *caracol* and the smoke of the *sahumador*. You can ask for up to four things. Mentally say, '*Ometeotl*.'

~ When you have finished this process, go down two heavens and back to the stars' heaven. Visualize the cosmos, find your own guiding star, which could be any, and make it shine more brightly so that you have a more fortunate life.

~ Contemplate your guiding star until you fall asleep.

I recommend that you repeat this exercise for 13 days from the new moon, so that you finish one day before the full moon and everything is perfectly synchronized with the cycles of the universe. Some months your requests will manifest and others not. You can repeat the procedure for those that haven't manifested during the next lunar cycle.

I hope all your dreams come down from the heavens for you.

When I attended Sergio's workshop, I asked Metztli, the moon, to make it possible for me to redecorate my house.

After a while, it totally slipped my mind. However, one day I changed a wardrobe. Then I got rid of a carpet. Next I had the kitchen, the living-room and the dining-room floors changed. Then I had all these rooms painted. Everything happened gradually and smoothly.

Sometime later I was rereading my notes on the workshop and realized all these changes had taken place in line with my request. At that moment Sergio's words hit me: 'Write down your requests, because we tend to forget them.'

DR PATRICIA QUINTOS, MEXICO CITY

Chapter 14

Tlahtollin: The Mathematical Order of Creation

Here is a fascinating technique I assembled by putting together several teachings based on Toltec numerology. It has produced the most extraordinary results.

As mentioned earlier, *tlahtolli* means 'word' in Náhuatl and *ollin* means 'movement'. *Tlahtollin* means 'the movement of the word that creates the mathematical order of creation'. It is a way of bringing together dreams, numerology and our relationship to the cosmos, the Earth and our own energetic system in order to manifest whatever we wish – perhaps a conscious death, lucid dreams, or more material items such as a job, a car and so forth. It can also be done for healing, including healing emotions.

I will explain the concept here as well as the way to perform the technique. Perform it for one thing at a time.

Exercise: Manifesting
through *Tlahtollin*

You can carry out this exercise at any time of the day. However, the best time would be at sunset.

∾ Sit down, facing east, and make yourself comfortable.

Ce, one

This is undoubtedly where we have to start in the process of manifestation. We have to put a new idea in the mind of Centeotl, primal energy, so that we can create what we desire.

∾ Choose the symbol you will assign to your manifestation. It could be anything that represents your desire, such as a flower or a hummingbird, but it has to be one you can remember, since you have to keep using it for the 13 days that the exercise lasts.

∾ Now, when you reach up and put your hands together above your head, you will reach a certain point. This is the point that joins the energy of Centeotl to your individual consciousness. So, raise your arms above your head and put your hands together to form a circle in which you visualize the symbol of your manifestation.

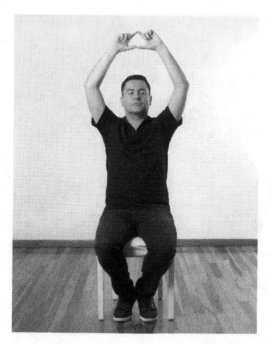

OME, TWO; OMITL, BONE

The second step consists of becoming a hollow bone, something Native Americans used to do, as they called their healers hollow bones. In the Mexican tradition, you are a hollow bone when you make the energy of Centeotl run through the cylinder of your body with all the wisdom on your ancestors.

~ Separate your hands and use them to form a cylinder around you from top to bottom.

~ Visualize that the energy of your symbol moves down through your body, crossing the centre of the cylinder until it reaches the Earth. The objective is to erase all the ancestral energy imprinted on your energetic bodies that could hinder your manifestation.

YEI, THREE; *YEZTLI*, BLOOD

The third step consists of allowing the energy streaming down from the symbol to the Earth to enter your blood and, through your bloodstream, flow through all your organs.

~ Visualize your blood carrying your intention through your body, through your organs, your being, your emotions. It lives inside you.

~ Remember that blood is the contact between *tonal* and *nahual*, and you are programming your waking and dreaming bodies with the same purpose.

NAHUI, FOUR; THE ORDER OF MOTHER EARTH

The fourth step consists of delivering the energy that now exists in the heavens, in your bones and in your blood to Mother Earth so that it can manifest there.

~ Visualize the blood carrying your intention moving to your left index finger.

~ Use your left index finger to draw the symbol of the four movements on the Earth so that they can manifest.

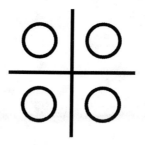

The four movements

In the original technique, you would prick your finger to fertilize the Earth with your blood. You can do it either way, but if you offer your bravery to Mother Earth, your reward will be greater.

In some communities, pricking the finger at New Year was a ritual for regeneration. The representative of the community would prick their finger and draw the symbol of the four movements on the Earth to ask for blessings for the new cycle.

This brings me to an important issue. Before the original rituals deteriorated, it was forbidden to use blood as an offering unless it was your own. I think all traditions started like this, but as time passed they started sacrificing animals or even people, a practice I strongly disagree with. I do not allow it, nor have I ever carried it out. I do, however, embrace the practice of giving some drops of my blood to Mother Earth, not only because of the beauty of offering the blood that gives me life but also because my blood represents the union of the moon and the Earth inside me.

Mahcuilli, FIVE

Mahcuilli, you will recall, has two different meanings: i) gripping something with your hands; ii) 'the worms in your hands', that is, your fingers. Step five reflects both meanings.

～ Point with the tips of the fingers of your left hand to the place where you drew the symbol and ask Tonantzin, Mother Earth, to allow you to manifest your desire. Ask her to give this energy to you by saying '*Xihualhui*' four times.

～ Feel the energy of your creation moving up from the Earth until it reaches your left hand. (Remember, you receive with the left hand and project with the right.)

Chicoacen, SIX; THE POWER OF THE SERPENT UNITED

The serpent represents energy, so the serpent united is one who moves up through the *totonalcayos* in a process similar to the rising of kundalini. This takes the energy you are receiving from the Earth to all your *totonalcayos*.

∽ As you are still receiving the energy from the Earth in your left hand, put your right hand on your coccyx and project that energy into your sacrum and then upwards through your genitals, navel, chest and neck until it comes out through your forehead in the form of a snake.

∽ Why through the forehead instead of the crown? Because the forehead chakra is the precious area for creation where *tonal* and *nahual* join. It is called precious because it takes its name from jade, the ancient Mexicans' most precious gemstone. Exiting through the crown is commonly used in enlightenment techniques or for conscious dying.

CHICOME, SEVEN; THE TWO SERPENTS UNITED

∽ The seventh step consists of visualizing the serpent coming out of your forehead dividing in two. One goes to the right and the other to the left, as far as they can.

∽ Let them go, then visualize them coming back, interweaving as they move right in front of your forehead.

∽ This is the sacred moment of creation. Say '*Ometeotl*.'

CHICUEY, EIGHT; THE FLOW OF THE ENERGY OF THE UNIVERSE

∽ The eighth step consists of asking what you want to manifest to come to you from the four cardinal points, or the petals of the flower, and from above and below. Ask the flow of the universe to bring it to you.

If this was all there was to it, manifestation would be very simple. And these steps may be enough. However, your underworlds, the places where your mind is trapped, may affect the process. If your underworlds and your inner enemy are very strong, you will always make bad decisions. For example, if you are asking for a partner to come into your life, you will choose the worst available, or even sabotage your chances of a relationship altogether. If a door opens, you will somehow manage to close it. If you come up with a new idea, you will discard it and say, 'No, I can't do it because I am too old.' Or you will make up thousands of other excuses not to do it.

It is for this reason that I recommend you carry out the *Teomanía* (*see pages 49–57*), or the healing exercises (*Part I*) before you start on the manifestation exercises. You can also go on to heal your underworlds in this exercise with the number nine.

CHICNAHUI, NINE; WHAT IS BURIED IN THE EARTH

In this step, you ask to heal the dreams that are preventing you from manifesting what you want, eliminate the destructive patterns in your life and overcome the obstacles on your path. Procrastination, lack of discipline and fear of change are the main obstacles that prevent manifestation from happening. These negative emotions consume your energy, preventing you from creating what you want and/or overcoming the view that it is difficult, or impossible, to achieve.

Symbolically, your destructive dreams, patterns and emotions all lie within your underworlds, within Mother Earth, a concept the Andeans also have, because they claim that the Pachamama, Mother Earth, takes care of our suffering until we can process it. Native Americans also have the same idea, as they hunt the soul inside Mother Earth.

So, if the underworlds lie inside Mother Earth, she is the one in charge of healing them. This is why the ninth step consists of asking her to heal your underworlds.

～ Draw the symbol of the four movements (*see page 167*) on the Earth, this time using your right hand. Once again, in the original technique you would prick your index finger and draw the symbol with a drop of your blood, offering your bravery in return for the changes you wanted to see.

～ Ask Tonantzin, Mother Earth, to heal all your underworlds.

MAHTLACTLI, 10; THE BACK OF THE HAND

This is used when you need to develop a talent in order to manifest something.

～ Put both hands together next to your face. Regardless of which side you put them, just spin them first on one side and then on the other, commanding that all the talents you need for that particular manifestation develop in your life.

As mentioned in the numerology chapter, using two hands (10 fingers) enables you to modify what you have been doing up to now, which was determined by the number nine.

MAHTLACTLI ONCE, 10 AND ONE: 11

If you have been able to change what you have been doing through step 10, then the time has come for you to change the path you are on.

∿ Hold your ankles with both hands (since symbolically you have already changed what you are doing).

∿ Ask your ankles to take your steps to the path of your new creation.

MAHTLACTLI OMOME, 10 AND TWO: 12; WISDOM

Here you are surrendering the old and starting a new cycle, a cycle full of wisdom.

∽ Put your hands on your knees with the aim of closing the cycle where you were unable to manifest what you were asking for and letting go of everything that needs to heal in your life.

∽ Stay in this position for about two minutes and feel the energy moving through your entire body, closing one cycle and opening a new one in your life.

Mahtlactli oneyi, **10** AND THREE: **13**; BLOOMING IN THE MOST BEAUTIFUL AND HARMONIOUS WAY

~ Take all the energy you created in the previous step up to your hips, because this is the place where sexual energy resides – the energy that can create anything in life.

~ Hold your hips on both sides and command that your sexual energy manifests your desire in a beautiful and harmonious way, as a flower does when it blooms.

~ To conclude, put your hands together and say:

Ometeotl. May [whatever you are asking for] manifest with the wisdom and the beauty of a flower. *Ometeotl.*

Do this exercise four times a day for 13 days. If you choose to prick your finger, you should only do it on the first movement of the day. For the other three movements, just draw the symbols.

If you are counting, you will realize you have repeated the exercise 52 times over the 13 days. New fire. New dreams.

Finally, to complement what you are doing, when you are lying in bed before you go to sleep, say:

> Tonight, I will dream about the symbol I chose for my manifestation.

If you dream of it and remember the dream, you can be sure that what you want to happen is about to manifest. If the manifestation happens first and you can't remember dreaming about the symbol, don't worry – you can be certain that you have already dreamed about it, otherwise the manifestation wouldn't be taking place.

If you want to accelerate the process, wait a while and then repeat the exercise. Try to start it during the dark of the moon or at new moon, so that the 13 days pass under a waxing moon.

I am Mexican, but I didn't know what that really meant until I studied the Toltec and Mexihca path. It has been an insightful healing journey of mystery, transformation, mindfulness, patience, faith and discipline. These teachings offer a way of transforming our lives by releasing old belief systems and blocks that keep us from being in peace, love and harmony with ourselves, others, and the world around us.

Following the practices has helped me resolve my problems and move through the energetic changes that I face on a daily basis in the fast-moving modern world. I am fascinated by the results of the rejuvenation exercises, which provide a simple path to let go of all that is not serving me and to bring myself in balance with my physical, mental, emotional and spiritual bodies. The healing modalities have cemented my connection with the elements and nature and provided me with the confidence to teach and heal others. The teachings have given me practical tools to create the connections needed to live a beautiful life, the life of my dreams.

Ometeotl.

Antoinette Gutierrez, Ozomacihuatl; San Diego, USA

CHAPTER 15

Tepeyolohtli: The Heart of the Mountains

I have left to last what I consider the pinnacle of the exploration of the caves of power, as well as the most powerful ritual of manifestation I know.

I'm very glad that I came across this ritual. My obsidian mirror teacher, Armando, described it as 'exploring the Tezcatlipoca path of darkness'. Darkness isn't negative in our tradition; it refers to the inner world, dreams and forces of the night, such as the moon. Exploring the path of darkness is the equivalent of a modern psychiatrist exploring the unconscious mind of a patient.

Armando explained that once we have worked with our own cave, the next step is to start working with the heart of the mountains, the *tepeyolohtli*. *Tepetl* means 'mountain' and *yolotl* 'heart'. In ancient Mexico the *tepeyolohtli* were groups of people.

The main objective of working with the heart of the mountains is to help others. It involves working with the caves of the mountains to help the collective mind.

In ancient Mexico, there were two groups of people who made pilgrimages to the mountains. Together they created the destiny of the collective. They could make it rain, create peace and prevent natural disasters from happening. Unfortunately, part of this knowledge has been lost. Nevertheless, Armando knew one of the rituals. In fact we were never able to perform together, but I took notes and later carried it out on my own and with my students, and I realized it was one of the most powerful rituals that could ever be performed.

As you may know, I am a man who loves cities, but over time I have learned to love nature too. I feel far better in cities, though, so the first time I tried this ritual I didn't do it in a cave in the mountains, I did it indoors at night, closing the blinds for complete darkness. Later it was amazing to realize that everything I had asked for in the ritual had manifested.

Subsequently I started teaching this ritual to my students. I used it not only for personal requests but also for collective ones. I asked for rain, the banning of genetically modified crops in Mexico, a decrease in the rate of violence in Monterrey, a city in the north of Mexico, and various other things. Coincidence or not, once again everything I asked for manifested.

Once, after I spoke about these experiences on one of my courses in Denver, Colorado, a man said to me, 'If you make it rain in New Mexico, where I live, I will believe everything you say.' So that morning we performed the ritual and in the evening it rained in New Mexico – only for half an hour, but it rained.

I would like to point out that he said, 'If *you* make it rain…' However, it wasn't down to me. I didn't make it rain, the forces we invoked in the ritual did. They deserve all the credit.

Of course, this ritual works far better if you perform it with a group, as then its power is augmented. That is why I am sharing one of the greatest treasures I have ever come across. I am sharing everything I was taught with respect and affection, so that you can use the heart of the mountains to create a better world.

EXERCISE: MANIFESTING THROUGH THE HEART OF THE MOUNTAINS

Go to a cave in the mountains, or find a pitch-black place where you can work. This ritual vibrates with the forces of the night. You can perform it in a cave on the first day and complete the rest of it at home if you wish. Of course, if you can perform it every day in a cave, that will be wonderful.

Decide what you want to manifest. You can make one, two or four requests, in alignment with the sacred mathematical system. I usually make two personal requests and two for the collective.

The only thing you need is a rattle or maraca.

~ Once you are inside the cave or dark place, kneel down, shaping your left hand as if it were a cup and holding the maraca in your right so that you can use it when it is time.

~ With force and authority, summon whatever you intend to manifest with the following words (I have left the most significant words in Náhuatl; you can say the rest in your native language):

> I summon [whatever you are summoning to manifest], as the son/daughter of Metztli (the moon),
>
> with the power of *Yohualli* [Jowalli] (the night),
>
> with the *Yayauhqui Tezcatlipoca* [Chey-shaow-ki Tezcatlipoca] (the Black *Tezcatlipoca*) as my witness,
>
> with the power of my Mother Tonantzin (Mother Earth).

~ Now order your desires to come to you by saying the words '*Maxite notzaqui* [Mashiti notzaki]', 'You are being called', four times and shaking the rattle as if it were a writhing snake. One of the meanings of the snake is the Earth, so you are asking what you want to manifest to come to Earth.

~ Carry out this procedure, from 'I summon' to '*Maxite notzaqui*', four times consecutively for each request you make.

~ Once you have finished, you will feel energy arriving. When this happens, start breathing through your mouth as if you were inhaling the smoke of Mrs Two's *copal* incense along with what you want to manifest.

~ Now blow it out into your left hand, the one you are holding in the shape of a cup.

~ Take the cup to your sternum, which represents the centre of *xochitl*, the flower, so that your manifestation blooms in a beautiful way. Then put your hands together and say:

> *Ometeotl.* May [what you are asking for] manifest with the beauty of the flower and the power of the cave.

I perform this ritual nine times, since that is the number of the Black Tezcatlipoca. If what I have asked for doesn't manifest, after a while I carry out a second cycle.

If you manage to gather a group for this ritual, your manifestations will be more powerful and at the same time you will be reviving one of the rituals that has almost been lost in ancient Mexico.

While at a workshop in the USA in the fall of 2012, Sergio taught the Tepeyolohtli manifestation ritual. After completing individual requests, he asked the group what they would like to create collectively. We chose several things: a good president (as elections were happening the following month); rain to ease the drought we had been experiencing for several years in Oregon (Sergio suggested this); and sustainable peace. We had not had a drop of rain for many months. What was amazing was that within two hours of the completion of the ritual the sky clouded up and it began to rain and continued raining for over three days.

In October 2015, Sergio returned and did the ritual again. While the results were not as dramatic this time, they were still impressive. We again asked for rain, and as soon as we had completed the ritual and walked outside for the closing ceremony, it began to drizzle. Granted, there were a few clouds in the sky, yet the weather forecast hadn't mentioned rain. The next day it rained heavily, with lightning and strong winds. The most remarkable occurrence of all has been that after many years western Oregon is no longer considered to be in a state of drought, according to the US Seasonal Drought Outlook Map.

VALERIE NIESTRATH, USA WORKSHOP ORGANIZER, APRIL 2016

PART IV

Enlightenment

CHAPTER 16

Blooming

The ancient Mexicans' word for what is known today as 'enlightenment' was 'blooming' or 'blossoming'. Why? Because it meant completing the entire flower: healing your ancestors, rejuvenating your body, manifesting your desires, aligning yourself with precious knowledge, healing your underworlds and having the will of a warrior. This can be written in a sentence, but was the work of a lifetime. To this day, it is something that many are striving for in one tradition or another, but few achieve.

Everything I have shared in this book has laid the foundation for blooming. If you have successfully demonstrated your power in tangible areas, like health and manifesting the life you want, the next step is to bloom. In this chapter I will share a basic technique for it and will take this further in other books. For now, I think this is an excellent beginning.

Xayaxolohtli: Xolotl's Mask, Quetzalcóatl's *Nahual*

This technique is part of the ancient Mexican art of dreaming. It consists of a very simple visualization that can change the course of your life, but first you need to understand some concepts.

In the Mexihca and Toltec tradition there is what is known as the long count, a period of 26,500 years, which, as with everything in this tradition, is based on the numerical order of the universe. So, in accordance with the four movements, the long count is divided into four periods of 6,625 years each, and these are called suns. At present the period of the Fifth Sun, Tecpatl Tonatiuh, the Sun of Flint, is about to give way to that of the Sixth Sun, Iztac Tonatiuh, the White Sun.

White is the colour of Quetzalcóatl, the Tezcatlipoca of knowledge and illumination. So this is the sun of precious knowledge. Cuauhtemoc, the last Aztec *tlahtoani*, council spokesman, ordered his people to keep their treasure safe because it would be recovered during the Sixth Sun. This is when we expect Quetzalcóatl to come back, not as a human being but as knowledge. The prophecy says Quetzalcóatls, plural, meaning people around the world will find this precious knowledge.

The following technique consists of manifesting the universe inside your cave in order to access precious knowledge. It seems quite simple, but it can bring enormous changes to your life if you practise it regularly.

EXERCISE: *XAYAXOLOHTLI*

⤳ Sit comfortably facing east, the direction of Quetzalcóatl.

⤳ Inhale through your nose, hold your breath and visualize the snake writhing up through all your *totonalcayos*:

- When it moves through your coccyx (*Colotl*), you are healing your ancestral patterns.

- When it moves through your genitals (*Ihuitl*), you are making your creations lighter.

- When it reaches your navel (*Pantli*), you are expressing the most favourable part of your birth chart and making changes in your life more easily.

- In your chest (*Xochitl*), you are moving towards your blossoming.

- In your neck (*Topilli*), you are recovering your power.

- At your forehead, the jade chakra (*Chalchiuhuitl*), you are bringing together the *tonal* and *nahual*.

⤳ To complete the process, when you reach the last *totonalcayo*, the crown, *Tecpatl*, spin it to change your destiny to one more favourable for enlightenment and then exhale.

⤳ Do this 12 times.

⤳ The 13th time is different. This time, once you reach your crown, instead of spinning it, when you exhale, come out through it in the form of the serpent.

- Now visualize yourself transforming into your favourite bird. If you are following the original technique, you will transform into a quetzal and soar to the sun.

- Visualize reaching Tonatiuh, Father Sun, asking to receive precious knowledge and transforming into Quetzalcóatl. (Those who know how to move the serpent upwards and bloom are the bearers of the precious knowledge.)

- When you have finished, put your hands together and say:

> *Ometeotl.* May life and precious knowledge bloom inside me. *Ometeotl.*

If you practise this technique every day, you can reach your destiny and bloom.

There are a lot more things to explore in this ancient tradition that has been slumbering, waiting for us, the people of the Sixth Sun, to bring it back to life. However, the practices I've outlined here will keep you pretty busy for a while.

Know that this book isn't in your hands by chance, but because somehow, either in your dreams or your unconscious mind, you have asked to heal and bloom through the knowledge of the ancient Mexicans.

Ometeotl. May all bloom. *Ometeotl.*

Acknowledgements

Honouring the ancient Mexican mathematics mentioned in this book, I would like to acknowledge all the forces and people who have helped me along the way:

Ce (One): Thanks to Centeotl, primal energy, which somehow came up with the idea of being transformed into this book, *Caves of Power*.

Ome (Two): To my two mothers, Maria del Carmen Gil and Rosa Hernández. One gave me magic and indigenous wisdom and the other the western mindset that has allowed me to present the ancient teachings in a way that works for the modern world.

Nahui (Four): To all the different lands that have received me and my teachings with friendship and love. Thanks to the UK, USA, Canada, Mexico, Italy, Spain, Turkey, Hungary, Sweden, the Netherlands, Argentina, Colombia and all the others that I've probably forgotten.

Mahcuilli (Five): To the five Tezcatlipocas. Inside and outside everything, you are always present in my life.

Chicome (Seven): To Michelle Pilley and Hay House, the power that has allowed me to manifest this creation.

Mahtlactli once (Eleven): To all the new paths to be opened, because I know this book will be a new cycle in my life.

Mahtlactli oneyi (Thirteen): To all my teachers. May your teachings, expressed in a modern way, blossom in the best way through this book.

ABOUT THE AUTHOR

Alexiara Oué

Sergio Magaña Ocelocoyotl is a well-known practitioner and teacher of the 5,000-year-old Toltec or Toltecayotl lineage of Mesoamerica. The tradition began with the ancient Chichimecas, who passed their knowledge to Teotihuacans and then the Toltecs, who then taught both the Mayans and Aztecs. Sergio is also trained in the Tol lineage of nahualism, dreaming knowledge that has been passed on in the oral tradition, without interruption, from master to student for 1,460 years. The time for these teachings to be unveiled is now, and Sergio is one of a few spokespeople asked to share this ancient and hidden wisdom with the world.

Sergio is the founder of Centro Energético Integral and the host of the radio show *The Sixth Sun*, which has aired in Mexico for 14 years. He speaks Spanish and English fluently, and has studied the mystical power of the Náhuatl language for many years. Sergio is a featured author in the book *Transforming Through 2012*, and author of *2012–2021: The Dawn of the Sixth Sun* and *The Toltec Secret*, both of which have been translated into numerous languages.

Sergio travels extensively and has a community of over 50,000 students in Mexico, the USA, Italy, the Netherlands, Sweden, Hungary, Canada, Spain and the UK. He lives in Mexico City and London.

www.sergiomagana.com

We hope you enjoyed this Hay House book. If you'd like to receive our online catalog featuring additional information on Hay House books and products, or if you'd like to find out more about the Hay Foundation, please contact:

Hay House, Inc., P.O. Box 5100, Carlsbad, CA 92018-5100
(760) 431-7695 or (800) 654-5126
(760) 431-6948 (fax) or (800) 650-5115 (fax)
www.hayhouse.com® • www.hayfoundation.org

———

Published in Australia by: Hay House Australia Pty. Ltd.,
18/36 Ralph St., Alexandria NSW 2015
Phone: 612-9669-4299 • *Fax:* 612-9669-4144
www.hayhouse.com.au

Published in the United Kingdom by: Hay House UK, Ltd.,
The Sixth Floor, Watson House, 54 Baker Street, London W1U 7BU
Phone: +44 (0)20 3927 7290 • *Fax:* +44 (0)20 3927 7291
www.hayhouse.co.uk

Published in India by: Hay House Publishers India,
Muskaan Complex, Plot No. 3, B-2, Vasant Kunj, New Delhi 110 070
Phone: 91-11-4176-1620 • *Fax:* 91-11-4176-1630
www.hayhouse.co.in

———

Access New Knowledge.
Anytime. Anywhere.

Learn and evolve at your own pace
with the world's leading experts.

www.hayhouseU.com